Contracts for Independent Readers
Historical Fiction

Grades 4–6

Writers:
Jan Brennan and Mary Sanford

Editor:
Kim T. Griswell

Contributing Editors:
Cindy K. Daoust and Cayce Guiliano

Art Coordinator:
Donna K. Teal

Artists:
Teresa R. Davidson, Sheila Krill, Kimberly Richard, Greg D. Rieves,
Rebecca Saunders, Barry Slate, Donna K. Teal

Cover Artists:
Nick Greenwood and Kimberly Richard

www.themailbox.com

©2000 by THE EDUCATION CENTER, INC.
All rights reserved.
ISBN #1-56234-406-4

Manufactured in the United States

10 9 8 7 6 5 4 3 2 1

Table of Contents

About This Book

What is historical fiction?

In historical fiction the reader is given a broad sense of particular events, feelings, or attitudes of the past. A historical novel takes place in a specific time in history or at a historical place. The characters may be real or fictional or a combination of both. The plot has a mixture of real and fictional events. The reader is left with a greater understanding of an event or place that has helped shape our world.

How to use this book:

Contracts for Independent Readers—Historical Fiction includes everything you will need to implement an independent reading program in your classroom.

The **Teacher's Organizational Checklist** on page 4 will help you monitor your students' progress throughout the year. To use this page, photocopy it to make a class supply and write each student's name in the space provided. Hold a conference with each student to assess the goals the student has for the semester or the year. Have the student write her goals in the space provided. Next, have each student choose one of the novels included in this book to read. List the title of the book in the appropriate column. When the student has completed an activity, write the date it was completed in the bottom portion of the corresponding box. Use the key at the bottom of the page to note the type of activity completed in the top portion of the corresponding box as shown in the sample. After evaluating the activities, write any comments you have in the space provided and have the student do the same. At the end of the semester or year, direct each student to complete the self-assessment portion detailing how she feels she has done at reaching her goals. Finally, write your own assessment of each student's progress.

The **introductory page** of each independent contract contains a description of the novel, background information on the author, and a student contract materials list. This list will aid you in preparing in advance any materials that students may need. Most of the listed materials can be found right in the classroom!

Each of the two programmable **contract pages** in each unit has six independent activities for students to choose from. Each unit also includes **reproducible pages** that correspond to several independent activities. The second contract page has slightly more advanced activities than the first contract page.

Since some novels are at higher reading levels or may contain more mature content, we suggest that you read each of the novels so that you may assist students in choosing which novels to read.

Also included in this book is a **student booklist** on page 61, which consists of 12 historical fiction novels, with a brief description of each. This list provides you with additional titles for students who finish early, for students who would enjoy reading other books in this genre, and for you to include in your classroom library.

Other Books in the Contracts for Independent Readers Series:
- *Contracts for Independent Readers—Humor*
- *Contracts for Independent Readers—Realistic Fiction*
- *Contracts for Independent Readers—Fantasy*
- *Contracts for Independent Readers—Adventure*
- *Contracts for Independent Readers—Mystery*

Book Title

Sample: Book Title

	Activity 1	Activity 2	Activity 3	Activity 4	Activity 5	Activity 6	Activity 7	Activity 8	Activity 9	Activity 10	Activity 11	Activity 12	Teacher Comments	Student Comments
MA 11/6	SS 11/7		LA 11/10											

Teacher Comments

Student Comments

Key
LA = Language Arts
RD = Reading
W = Writing
MA = Math
SS = Social Studies
SC = Science
A = Art
MU = Music
RS = Research
CT = Critical Thinking

Student Goals:

Self-Assessment:

Teacher Assessment:

Sarah, Plain and Tall
by Patricia MacLachlan

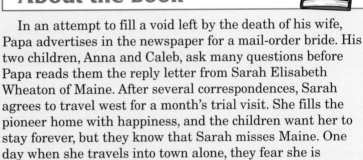

About the Book

In an attempt to fill a void left by the death of his wife, Papa advertises in the newspaper for a mail-order bride. His two children, Anna and Caleb, ask many questions before Papa reads them the reply letter from Sarah Elisabeth Wheaton of Maine. After several correspondences, Sarah agrees to travel west for a month's trial visit. She fills the pioneer home with happiness, and the children want her to stay forever, but they know that Sarah misses Maine. One day when she travels into town alone, they fear she is leaving them. To their great relief, Sarah returns with a gift, a smile, and the assurance that even though she misses her home by the sea, she would miss Anna, Caleb, and Papa even more.

About the Author

Patricia MacLachlan was born on March 3, 1938, in Cheyenne, Wyoming, and was raised in Minnesota. Eventually she moved east, where she graduated from the University of Connecticut in 1962. She lives in Williamsburg, Massachusetts, with her husband, Robert.

MacLachlan published her first book in 1979 after

teaching English for 16 years. She has written many books over the years, including *Arthur for the Very First Time*, and *Cassie Binegar*. Her book ideas originate from her family life, both past and present. Her characters talk to her, and then she begins to write about them. She does not use an outline, and she often does not know how the story will end. "My inspiration for writing is all the wonderful books that I read as a child and that I still read." Her advice to children who want to become authors is to read, read, read, and to choose many different books. Then write every day whether you feel like it or not. This is how to develop your craft.

Student Contract Materials List

- Activity #1:   copy of page 8
- Activity #2:   tape recorder, blank tape
- Activity #3:   white construction paper, paints
- Activity #4:   copy of page 9
- Activity #5:   reference materials on pioneer food, 3 paper plates, food pyramid, crayons or markers
- Activity #6:   drawing paper, charcoal pencil or lead pencil, colored pencils
- Activity #7:   paper and pencil
- Activity #8:   art reference books, art materials
- Activity #9:   copy of page 10
- Activity #10:   local street map, paper
- Activity #11:   tape recorder, blank tape
- Activity #12:   poster board, art supplies reference materials on railroads

Sarah, Plain and Tall
Independent Contract

Name:_____ Number of activities to be completed: _____

1. Writing

Patricia MacLachlan was awarded the 1986 Newbery Medal for her exceptional writing in *Sarah, Plain and Tall*. Writers often use crisp adjectives, choice words, and all five senses to paint descriptive word pictures for their readers. Obtain a copy of page 8 from your teacher. Refer to chapter 8 for a description of the squall that struck the farm. Choose sensory details about the squall to fill in the blanks on the chart. Next, think about a storm that you have experienced and add sensory descriptions to the chart. Use the words from the chart to write a paragraph about your storm.

2. Music

In the beginning of the book, Caleb asks Anna about their mother's songs, hoping they will help him remember Mama. Think about a favorite childhood song, such as a bedtime song, a silly song, or one your family sang together. Record yourself singing your favorite song or perform the song for the class. If desired, invite friends or family to join in the recording session or performance.

3. Art

When neighbor Maggie comes for a visit, she gives Sarah a wooden box filled with plants, such as zinnias, marigolds, and wild feverfew. It reminds Sarah of her garden of dahlias, columbine, and nasturtiums in Maine. Maggie tells Sarah that she must have a garden wherever she is living. Paint Sarah's Maine garden on one half of a large sheet of white construction paper. Paint her prairie garden on the other half. Add background scenery on each half to represent each setting.

4. Language Arts

Sarah has many necessary skills for life on the prairie. In pioneer days, people with many skills had the best chance for survival. To investigate how life has changed since the pioneer days, interview three people (one your age, one about 30 years older than you, and one about 60 years older than you) about their skills. Obtain a copy of page 9 from your teacher. Use it to record your interviewees' responses. Compare the three generations' skills with the list of Sarah's skills. Have a discussion with classmates about the differences between the skills of each generation.

5. Social Studies

In the story, Sarah makes stew and Papa bakes bread for dinner. A pioneer family had to raise or grow most of its own food. Research some of the foods a family living on the prairie might have eaten. Obtain three paper plates and then illustrate a prairie breakfast on the first plate, a prairie lunch on the second plate, and a prairie supper on the third plate. Be sure to include a variety of foods. Obtain a food pyramid to check whether each plate contains a balanced meal.

6. Art

One day Sarah makes a charcoal drawing of the prairie fields that remind her of the rolling sea waves. Caleb notices that the colors of the sea (blue, green, and gray) are missing from the drawing. Later, Sarah buys three colored pencils for everyone to use. Caleb is thrilled that she has brought the sea to them. Use a charcoal pencil or lead pencil to draw a scene of something special. Then add subtle touches of color to liven it up.

Sarah, Plain and Tall
Independent Contract

Name:_____ Number of activities to be completed: _____

Writing

In the beginning of the book, Caleb asks Anna to retell the story of his birth. Many families have the tradition of passing on stories of incidents in their children's lives. This is an example of oral tradition. Write down a story about yourself or a family member that has been told to you. Practice telling the story out loud, and then tell it to your classmates.

Art Research

Sarah travels from the coast of Maine to the prairies of the Midwest. Compare the two areas by researching artwork from the pioneer time period. Consider Winslow Homer, known for painting Maine seascapes, and Grant Wood, known for painting midwestern farms. Using reference books, prepare a display of each artist's work, including a brief description of each picture.

Language Arts

Sarah brings simple gifts of natural beauty from the sea: a moon snail for Caleb and a sea stone for Anna. What are some nature items from your state that you consider beautiful? Obtain a copy of page 10 from your teacher. Select one natural item and write a haiku, cinquain, and diamonte poem about it.

Geography

Caleb and Anna live three miles away from their school. During winter Papa drives them to school when the snow is very deep. Determine the distance between your home and your school by using the map scale on your town's street map. Then draw a map that shows the route, including details such as buildings and landmarks.

Language Arts

Imagine that Sarah returned to Maine to visit her brother William. Write a monologue (a long speech given by one person) including what Sarah might have said to William to describe her new home and family. Include a comparison between her midwestern home and William's coastal home. Practice your speech using a tape recorder. Then perform the speech for your classmates.

Research

Sarah tells Jacob that she will come by train from her home in Maine to their farm in the Midwest. Pioneer travel was not easy, but the train made traveling long distances more desirable. Research the first railroads in America. Investigate when the first rails were laid, when they connected America from coast to coast, and some of the uses of railroads. Create a poster showing the history of the American railroad.

Sensing a Storm

Five Senses	Prairie Squall	My Storm Experience
Hearing		
Seeing		
Smelling		
Feeling		
Tasting		

My Storm Experience

_____

_____

_____

_____

_____

_____

_____

Note to the teacher: Use with activity #1 on page 6.

Four Generations

Name: Sarah Wheaton

Generation: early 1900s

Skills:

making stew

giving haircuts

gardening

drawing

singing

reading

writing

fixing the roof

plowing the field

driving the wagon

Name: _____

Generation: _____

Skills:

_____

_____

_____

_____

_____

_____

_____

_____

Glue a photo or drawing of the interviewee here.

Name: _____

Generation: _____

Skills:

_____

_____

_____

_____

_____

_____

_____

_____

Glue a photo or drawing of the interviewee here.

Name: _____

Generation: _____

Skills:

_____

_____

_____

_____

_____

_____

_____

_____

Glue a photo or drawing of the interviewee here.

Note to the teacher: Use with activity #4 on page 6.

Nature-Inspired Poetry

Haiku Sample

Moon Snail

Seagulls pick you up.
Drop you down from up above.
Dinnertime has come.

Diamonte

| 1 noun |
| 2 adjectives |
| 3 verbs |
| 4 nouns |
| 3 verbs |
| 2 adjectives |
| 1 noun |

Diamonte Sample

Shells
Mysterious, beautiful
Rolled, pushed, carried
Gifts, treasures, nature, houses
Sheltered, protected, housed
Cozy, quiet
Homes

Haiku

| 5 syllables |
| 7 syllables |
| 5 syllables |

Cinquain

| 2 syllables (one word) |
| 4 syllables (describing subject) |
| 6 syllables (feeling phrase) |
| 8 syllables (feeling phrase) |
| 2 syllables (renaming subject) |

Seastone
Tumbled, polished
Feels so smooth in my hand
Fits so perfectly in my palm
Seastone

Cinquain Sample

Note to the teacher: Use with activity #9 on page 7.

Number the Stars

by Lois Lowry

About the Book

Number the Stars takes place in 1943. Germany occupies Denmark, and Jewish people, like Ellen Rosen and her family, aren't safe. Many *Danes,* or people from Denmark, risk their lives helping Jewish friends and neighbors hide or escape to Sweden. Through the support of the Danish resistance movement and Annemarie's family, Ellen and her parents travel to Annemarie's uncle's farm. There they gather with a small group of other Jews to prepare for their dangerous escape. Hidden in a secret compartment on a boat, the Jews are smuggled to Sweden and safety. Annemarie discovers she has the courage and bravery to risk her life for a friend and for a cause in which she believes.

About the Author

Lois Lowry was born on March 20, 1937, the second of three children of Robert and Katharine Hammersberg. Lowry always felt lucky to be a middle child, for it was a position in the family that allowed her time to read and develop her imagination. Her father was an army dentist, so the family traveled all over the world with him. Born in Hawaii, Lowry experienced life and people in many places, including Japan, Pennsylvania, New York, and Washington, DC.

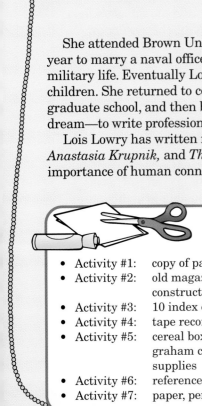

She attended Brown University in Rhode Island but left after her sophomore year to marry a naval officer and once again follow the busy traveling circuit of military life. Eventually Lowry and her husband settled in Maine and raised four children. She returned to college at the University of Southern Maine, went to graduate school, and then began a career that had been her childhood dream—to write professionally.

Lois Lowry has written more than 20 novels, such as *A Summer to Die, Anastasia Krupnik,* and *The Giver.* She feels that all her books deal with the importance of human connections.

Student Contract Materials List

- Activity #1:   copy of page 14
- Activity #2:   old magazines, scissors, glue, construction paper
- Activity #3:   10 index cards
- Activity #4:   tape recorder, blank tape
- Activity #5:   cereal boxes, building blocks, or graham crackers; arts-and-crafts supplies
- Activity #6:   reference materials on the seasons
- Activity #7:   paper, pencil

- Activity #8:   several fairy tales
- Activity #9:   world map, copy of page 15, crayons or markers
- Activity #10: construction paper, crayons or markers
- Activity #11: construction paper, glue, arts-and-crafts supplies
- Activity #12: old magazines, construction paper, scissors, glue, crayons or markers

11

Number the Stars

Independent Contract

Name:_____ Number of activities to be completed: _____

---

 1. | **Math**

Most countries have their own system of money. The United States has the dollar and Denmark has the krone. Obtain a copy of page 14 from your teacher. Complete the page as directed to compare the dollar and the krone.

 2. | **Social Studies**

In chapter 1, Mrs. Rosen tells the girls, "It is important to be one of the crowd, always." Think about what she might mean by that statement. Then do the following activity to see what a difference it makes to be one of the crowd. Cut 15 face pictures from old magazines. Glue the faces, grouped together in a crowd, onto half a sheet of construction paper. Cut and glue three more faces to the other half of the paper. Look at the paper for one minute; then turn it over. Which faces can you remember in detail? Which are harder to remember? Share this activity with the class and explain your findings.

 3. | **Language Arts**

Historical fiction combines historical facts with fiction. The characters, although based on real people, are usually fictitious, as are some of the details. The basis for the story, however, is usually factual. Lois Lowry explains in the afterword where fact ends and fiction begins. Carefully reread this section. Then make a set of ten fact or fiction cards based on this information. Write each statement and page number on the front of a card and "fact" or "fiction" on the back. For example, "Denmark surrendered to Germany in 1940" and "Page 133" on the front and "Fact" on the back.

 4. | **Language Arts**

Peter Neilsen and Annemarie's older sister, Lise, are part of the Danish resistance movement. This organization was composed mostly of young, brave people whose courageous acts saved the lives of thousands of Danish Jews. If you could have talked to Peter or Lise before they died, what would you have asked them? Write five to ten questions and the answers they might have given. Then conduct an interview with one of them by reading both parts, changing your voice to be both the interviewer and the interviewee. If possible, tape-record your interview.

 5. | **Art**

Annemarie's little sister, Kirsti, loves stories about kings, queens, and castles. Denmark has several castles, such as Amalienborg (King Christian X's castle), and Kronberg Castle. Research several castles, including what they look like and what they are made from. Then build a model of a castle, using materials such as cereal boxes, building blocks, graham crackers, and other arts-and-crafts supplies.

 6. | **Science**

Winter nights in Scandinavia (Denmark, Norway, and Sweden) are dark and long. This is because of the countries' locations on the earth. Research to figure out why this is true. Then use your imagination and the facts you gathered about Scandinavia's long winter to write and illustrate a short story about what you would do for fun on a long, dark night.

Number the Stars
Independent Contract

Name:_____ Number of activities to be completed: _____

 7. | **Language Arts**

In chapter 2, Annemarie's papa tells how King Christian is so loved by all of his people that any Danish citizen would give up his life to protect him. Think about the people of the United States. Do you think they feel the same about the president? Write a short play in which the characters discuss whether or not they would give up their lives to save the president's life and why.

 8. | **Writing**

Kirsti, Annemarie's younger sister, loves having Annemarie tell her fairy tales. Fairy tales generally are short, funny, and end happily. Good is rewarded, and evil is punished. Wishes come true. Often, the youngest or smallest succeeds, where as the oldest or largest is defeated. Reread some of your favorite fairy tales, keeping these general characteristics in mind. Then write an original fairy tale starring yourself or one of the characters in the book as the main character.

 9. | **Social Studies**

Denmark was occupied by German soldiers during World War II. This caused many Jewish people, like the Rosens, to flee to safety in Sweden. Study a world map to find the location of these three countries (Denmark, Germany, and Sweden). Then obtain a copy of page 15 from your teacher. Complete the map at the top of the page and then answer the questions that follow to learn more about the places that play a major role in the lives of the Rosens and Johansens.

 10. | **Language Arts**

Annemarie and Ellen do without many foods in Copenhagen during the war. However, when the girls visit Uncle Henrik, they are able to enjoy some treats. Use the book to make a list of foods the Johansens and the Rosens are not able to eat or wish they could eat during Germany's occupation. Then make a second list of foods they are able to eat at Uncle Henrik's farm. Use these foods to design an illustrated menu for the girls to choose from when the war is over!

 11. | **Writing**

The way we look gives clues about who we are. The soldiers pick out Ellen's dark hair because Danes are commonly light-haired people. However, our appearance does not tell what kind of person we are inside. Write a poem about living in a world with many different kinds of people. Use a sheet of construction paper and arts-and-crafts supplies to make a frame for your poem. Glue your poem in the center of your frame.

 12. | **Art**

The Danish resistance movement had a strong role in saving thousands of Jewish people during World War II. These people were extremely brave. Do you think Annemarie was brave? What is your definition of brave? Create a collage of magazine pictures, your own drawings, and words that represent what bravery means to you.

Name _____

14

Dollars to Kroner

I. When tourists travel from one country to another, they must exchange their money for the money used in that country. An American traveling in Denmark has to exchange American dollars for Danish kroner (DKr). Practice converting the price of the items below into kroner, using the following conversion rate.

Conversion rate: $1.00 = about 8 DKr (kroner)

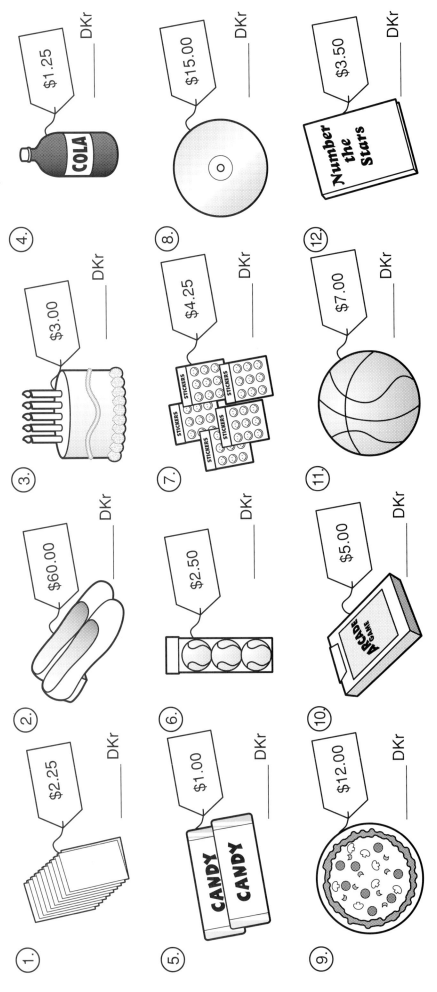

1. $2.25 _____ DKr

2. $60.00 _____ DKr

3. $3.00 _____ DKr

4. $1.25 _____ DKr

5. $1.00 _____ DKr

6. $2.50 _____ DKr

7. $4.25 _____ DKr

8. $15.00 _____ DKr

9. $12.00 _____ DKr

10. $5.00 _____ DKr

11. $7.00 _____ DKr

12. $3.50 _____ DKr

II. On the back of this sheet, draw five objects you would like to buy. Then write the cost of each object in dollars and kroner.

Note to the teacher: Use with activity #1 on page 12. Conversion rate current as of April 2000.

Where in Denmark?

Many important places are mentioned in *Number the Stars.* Use the directions and map below to find the places the Johansens and Rosens visit or see on their way to Uncle Henrik's farm. Then use the map to answer the questions at the bottom of the page.

Directions:

1. Circle Copenhagen, the home of the Johansens and Rosens, with a red crayon.
2. Draw a purple triangle around Gilleleje, Uncle Henrik's hometown.
3. Draw a green square around Helsingor, where Kirsti sees the castle from the train.
4. Circle Odense, the home of Hans Christian Andersen, with a yellow crayon.
5. Trace the Germany-Denmark border with an orange crayon.
6. Color the Kattegat, or part of the North Sea, blue.

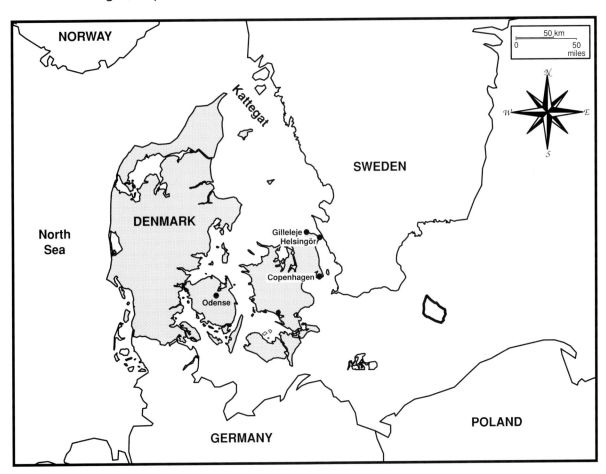

Questions:

1. What direction is Copenhagen from the German border? _____

2. Is Sweden closer to Germany or Denmark? _____

3. Name at least four different ways a person could travel to Sweden from Denmark. (Be creative.) _____

4. If you could live anywhere in Denmark, where would you choose? _____

_____

Out of the Dust
by Karen Hesse

About the Book

Billie Jo Kelby is almost 14 years old when she begins keeping a journal about her life growing up during the Great Depression in Oklahoma. Her compelling story, told in free verse, highlights the frustrations and crushing hardships of surviving the smothering heat, choking dust, and destructive winds of Oklahoma's dust bowl. Billie Jo's dream of becoming a pianist is almost completely lost when a horrible accident claims the life of her pregnant mother and terribly scars her own hands. Left alone with her grieving, silent father, Billie Jo struggles to make sense out of the terrible things her family has been through. Just as she is ready to leave the dust bowl behind her, she reaches deep within herself and finds the inner strength to reclaim her hopes and dreams.

About the Author

Karen Hesse was born on August 29, 1952, in Baltimore, Maryland. Growing up, an apple tree and the public library were refuges that provided her with the privacy she needed to read. Along with a great love of reading, Hesse had an active imagination. At one point in her childhood, she was sure she could fly and was prepared to prove it until her mother stopped her.

During high school, Hesse became involved in drama. She continued with drama at Towson State College, but left college and the stage after two years to marry Randy Hesse. She later completed her undergraduate work at the University of Maryland.

From the time she was ten years old, Hesse knew she was good with words. She has used experiences from her childhood and family experiences in her stories. *Letters From Rifka* is based on the experiences of her great-aunt. Hesse was advised not to write historical fiction, but she followed her heart and her love for research anyway, and in 1998 she won the Newbery Award for *Out of the Dust*!

Student Contract Materials List

- **Activity #1:** shoebox, arts-and-crafts supplies
- **Activity #2:** 2 sheets of 12" x 18" light-colored construction paper, crayons or markers
- **Activity #3:** copy of page 19, 1 sheet of 8½" x 11" poster board, 2 sheets of 8½" x 11" white paper
- **Activity #4:** reference materials on the dust bowl
- **Activity #5:** 1 sheet of 12" x 18" light-colored construction paper, reference materials on volcanoes, crayons or markers
- **Activity #6:** reference materials on apple pandowdy, recipe books, 1 sheet of 9" x 12" red construction paper, scissors

- **Activity #7:** pencil, paper
- **Activity #8:** reference materials on Dorothea Lange and Walker Evans, 5 sheets of 8½" x 11" white paper, 5 index cards
- **Activity #9:** copy of page 20, crayons or markers
- **Activity #10:** reference materials on grasshoppers, 1 sheet of 12" x 18" light-colored construction paper, markers
- **Activity #11:** reference materials on ragtime music, several recordings of ragtime music
- **Activity #12:** reference materials on windmills, craft sticks, cardboard, other building materials

Out of the Dust
Independent Contract

Name:_____ Number of activities to be completed: _____

 ### 1. Language Arts

Billie Jo has two boxes in her closet filled with precious mementos of her life. Reread "Boxes," September 1934, to discover what she keeps in her special boxes. Then use arts-and-crafts supplies to design a special box of your own! Gather several items that have special meaning to you, and place them in the box. On a slip of paper, write a sentence about each item, telling what it is and why you chose it. Attach each slip to the corresponding item in your box.

 ### 2. Art

Billie Jo writes that President Roosevelt wants people to plant trees to help solve the problems of the dust bowl. He says trees will break the wind, help end the drought, and hold on to the land. Billie Jo's parents have an argument about the amount of water Ma's two apple trees need to survive. Imagine having to make the decision whether or not to plant trees on your farm. Design two billboards, one advertising the benefits of planting trees and the other explaining the negative aspects of planting trees.

 ### 3. Math

While Billie Jo's mother is pregnant with one baby, Oliva Dionne gives birth to five babies! In a sense, she also gave birth to the word *quintuplets* because her babies were the first known quintuplets to live more than a few hours after birth. There are several words that have the Latin base *quintus,* meaning fifth. Obtain a copy of page 19 from your teacher to make a book of fives.

 ### 4. Social Studies

Imagine that you can change the course of history by traveling back in time. Reread "The Path of Our Sorrow," September 1934, about some of the incidents that led to the dust bowl. Then research the causes of the dust bowl. Use the information you find to write a speech. Prepare the speech as if you had gone back in time to Oklahoma in the 1920s. Warn the people about the future tragedy of the dust bowl, and give them suggestions as to how they can avoid it.

 ### 5. Science

When Billie Jo mentions that a volcano erupted in Hawaii, she suggests that it was something like a dust storm. Reread "Fields of Flashing Light," March 1934, and "Dust Storm," March 1935, in which Billie Jo describes the dust storms. Research volcanoes to compare and contrast them with dust storms. Then divide a sheet of construction paper in half. On one half, draw pictures and write a paragraph describing dust storms. On the other half, draw pictures and write a paragraph describing volcanic eruptions.

 ### 6. Language Arts

Billie Jo longs to have apples from Ma's trees to make all sorts of apple treats, such as apple pie, applesauce, and apple cobbler. When Sheriff Robertson confiscates one thousand pounds of sugar, he gives some of it to Billie Jo's teacher and tells her to bake apple pandowdy for her students. Research apple pandowdy to find out how it is made. Next, cut out five construction paper apple shapes. Write the recipe for apple pandowdy on one shape. Then look up the recipes for four of your favorite apple treats and write them on each of the other apple shapes. Staple the shapes together to create an apple-shaped recipe book!

Out of the Dust

Independent Contract

Name:_____ Number of activities to be completed: _____

 7. **Language Arts**

Out of the Dust is written in *free verse,* a type of poetry that has no set rhythm or rhyme. Reread "Thanksgiving List," November 1935. Then compile a list of ideas or things for which you are thankful. Using Billie Jo's poem as a model, write your own poem of thanksgiving in free verse form.

 8. **Art**

Even amidst the struggles of living through the dust bowl years, some things still bring enjoyment. Billie Jo finds enjoyment in art ("Art Exhibit," December 1934). She views the exhibit three times, and when it is gone, she misses it. Research Dorothea Lange and Walker Evans, famous photographers during the 1930s. Prepare an art exhibit for your class by drawing five pictures that show the life described by Billie Jo and shown in the photographs of Lange and Evans. Make an index card for each picture, giving it a title and telling what it is about.

 9. **Social Studies**

Billie Jo never identifies the town where she lives, but there are references that help to place it. Billie Jo's family lives in a "Panhandle shack" and Aunt Ellis lives in Lubbock, Texas, which is "a ways south of here." Obtain a copy of page 20 from your teacher and then study the map to become familiar with the area where Billie Jo is from. After studying the map, complete the page as directed.

 10. **Science**

Billie Jo describes grasshoppers coming and devouring plant life. Research grasshoppers to find out what they eat, their life cycle, and any other interesting information. Draw a diagram of a grasshopper and label its parts. Then write a story about grasshoppers under the picture, using the information you have gathered.

 11. **Music**

One source of entertainment for people during the dust bowl years was music. When Billie Jo plays ragtime, or a rag, on the piano, it makes the crowd happy. Research ragtime music to find out why it was called rag and how it is different from other music. Check out several ragtime recordings from your local library. Then write a review of ragtime that could be included in your local newspaper. Play some rag for your classmates and ask them their opinions of the music. Compare their reviews with your own.

 12. **Science**

Billie Jo's dad spends many hours digging a pond and repairing the windmill. Ma had wanted the windmill to provide water for her apple trees. Research windmills to find out how they are built, how they work, and where they get their energy. Then build a miniature windmill using craft sticks, cardboard, and other materials.

Name _____

Fives Aplenty!

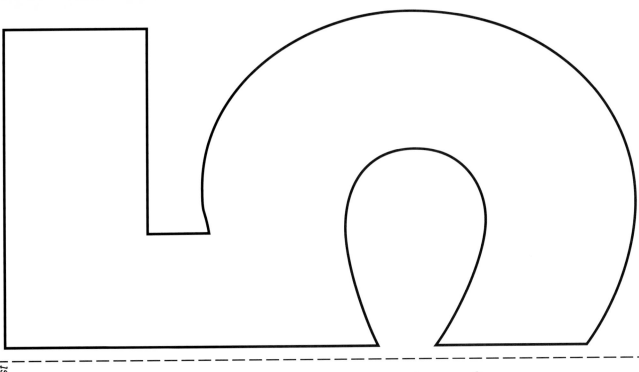

I. Read the words below that are based on the Latin word *quintus*. Then read each definition. Match each word to its definition. Use a dictionary to help you.

1. quintet

2. quintile

3. quintuple

4. quintuplets

5. quintuplicate

a. an adjective meaning to consist of five parts

b. a noun in statistics meaning one-fifth of a total sample

c. a verb meaning multiplied by five

d. a noun meaning a composition for five voices or instruments

e. a noun meaning five offspring born in a single birth

II. Cut out the number five pattern. Then trace the five twice onto poster board and four times onto white drawing paper. Cut out the fives. Decorate the poster board fives as the front and back covers. Write a different word from above on the top of each paper five, draw an illustration of the word in the vertical part of the five, and write the definition of the word around the curve of the five. Create a book of fives by placing the five pages between the front and back covers and stapling the fives along the left edge.

Note to the teacher: Use with activity #3 on page 17.

Where in the Oklahoma Panhandle?

Many places in Oklahoma are mentioned in *Out of the Dust.* Follow the directions below to locate each place on the map.

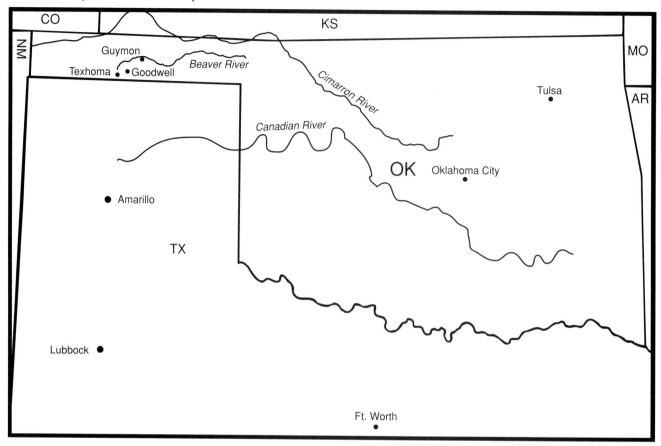

1. Locate the Oklahoma Panhandle and color it yellow.

2. Why do you think this area is called the Panhandle? _____
   _____
   _____

3. Aunt Ellis is from Lubbock, Texas. Find Lubbock and circle it in red.

4. Locate the states that border the Panhandle. Trace the borders of these states in purple where they touch the Panhandle.

5. Arley Wanderdale and his Black Mesa Boys have connections in Goodwell and Texhoma. Locate these two towns and circle them in green.

6. Joe De La Flor drives his cattle past the Beaver River to the Cimarron River. Find these rivers on the map and trace them in blue.

7. Mad Dog is going to sing on the radio in Amarillo, Texas. Circle Amarillo in orange.

8. Do you think the Oklahoma Panhandle is a good name for this area? _____
   If you could change the name, what would you change it to and why? _____
   _____
   _____

Roll of Thunder, Hear My Cry
by Mildred D. Taylor

About the Book

Through the story of the Logan family, *Roll of Thunder, Hear My Cry* illustrates how hard the 1930s were for many Black Americans. The Logan family has a closeness that gives them the strength to deal with the injustices surrounding them. Papa advises each member of the family to think of the consequences of his or her actions before reacting to unfair treatment because sometimes the consequences are far worse than the injustice. Work was scarce and many Black Americans were caught in the hopeless cycle of poverty brought about by sharecropping. To the Logans, owning their own land was the key to their freedom.

About the Author

Mildred D. Taylor was born on September 13, 1943, in Jackson, Mississippi, and was exposed to discrimination at a very young age. Her father, to whom she dedicates this book, moved the family to Toledo, Ohio, after being outraged by several incidents of racism. He wanted a new and better life in the North, while keeping his family roots alive with frequent trips back to the South. Here Mildred saw firsthand the many signs of segregation on which she based her writings.

Taylor's schooling began in an elementary school where she was the only black student. She felt she had to do her best because she felt that she represented not only herself, but also her family and her race. Going to high school in the North, she felt removed from the civil rights movement, but she was aware of the issues. She then attended college at the University of Toledo. Initially, Taylor based her writing style on authors she loved, such as Charles Dickens, but found these styles stiff and unnatural for her. Finally, after some time in the Peace Corps she enrolled in the Graduate School of Journalism at the University of Colorado. Taylor's first book featuring the Logan family was *Song of the Trees*. This was followed by *Roll of Thunder, Hear My Cry,* for which she was awarded the Newbery Medal. She continued the Logan family saga with four more books, all compelling and memorable.

Student Contract Materials List

- Activity #1: *Aesop's Fables,* crayons or markers, white paper
- Activity #2: reference materials on the United States
- Activity #3: 11 index cards, string, hole puncher, crayons or markers
- Activity #4: fabric pieces, black felt, glue, reference materials on quilts
- Activity #5: reference materials on Rosa Parks
- Activity #6: copy of page 24
- Activity #7: reference materials on cotton, 1 sheet of 8½" x 11" white paper
- Activity #8: copy of page 25
- Activity #9: copy of page 26
- Activity #10: cereal boxes or craft sticks, reference materials on tree houses, glue, scissors, markers, various art supplies
- Activity #11: reference materials on fire fighting, poster board
- Activity #12: ruler, crayons or markers

Roll of Thunder, Hear My Cry

Independent Contract

Name:_____ Number of activities to be completed: _____

1. Language Arts

The Logan children are excited to receive new books for Christmas. Christopher-John and Little Man each receive a volume of *Aesop's Fables*. A *fable* is a brief tale which often includes animals that speak and act like humans to teach a lesson. Locate a collection of *Aesop's Fables*. Read two or three of the fables, noticing the problem, how it is solved, and the lesson being taught. Then write your own fable about your favorite part in *Roll of Thunder, Hear My Cry* and illustrate it.

2. Social Studies

One night when Cassie can't fall asleep she challenges herself to name all the states geographically. Her teacher, Miss Crocker, usually asks the class to name the states alphabetically, but Cassie wants a tougher challenge. Come up with an easy way to remember the names of the states in any order you choose. Write the directions explaining your method and then offer to teach it to the class.

3. Writing

Cassie and her family eat many special foods, such as those mentioned in chapter seven and in chapter ten. Choose ten of the foods mentioned to create a recipe book. On each of ten index cards write the name of the food, the ingredients you think would be used in preparing it, directions on how you would prepare it, and an illustration of the finished product. Then, using an additional index card, create a cover by adding a title, the author (your name), and an illustration. Punch two holes in the index cards and tie a piece of string loosely in each hole to complete your recipe book.

4. Art

In chapter 3, Cassie's patchwork quilt helps keep her warm in bed. Research quilts to learn how the squares are arranged. Then make a quilt piece by choosing several pieces of fabric and arranging them on a piece of black felt. Once you have them arranged, glue the fabric to the felt. Write a short paragraph explaining why you chose that particular fabric and design. Glue your paragraph to the back of your quilt piece. Then hang it from the ceiling for everyone to enjoy.

5. Research

This novel tells the struggles of a few black families in the South in the early 1930s. The Logans are trying to help bring about change for Black Americans. Many people working toward that same goal contributed to the civil rights movement. Research Rosa Parks and her impact on the civil rights movement. Think about what might have motivated Rosa Parks and whether or not the Logan family would have considered her a hero. Write a letter from Cassie's point of view to Rosa Parks, telling Ms. Parks how you feel about everything she accomplished for Black Americans.

6. Science

As chapter 9 opens, it is springtime and Cassie's heart soars as she witnesses all the signs of new life. Reread the first two paragraphs of chapter nine, noting the descriptions dealing with spring. Obtain a copy of page 24 from your teacher and complete it as directed.

Roll of Thunder, Hear My Cry

Independent Contract

Name:_____ Number of activities to be completed: _____

7. Research

Much of the land, which is vital to Cassie's family, is used for growing cotton. Research cotton; then choose one of the many cotton products and write a "life history" of it. Begin with its birth (how it is grown and cultivated) and chronicle the special events in its life (where it is raised, or grown, and how it is made into what it is today). Then design a pamphlet detailing your product's life.

8. Math

Many of the farmers who live near Cassie are sharecroppers. Sharecropping involved two people—the *tenant farmer,* who worked the land, and the *landlord,* who owned the land. This was usually a no-win situation for the farmer who was trapped into a binding deal where he often ended up owing more than he earned to the landlord. At the end of chapter 4, Mr. Turner is explaining to Cassie's mother why he can't afford to shop in Vicksburg. Reread the last two pages of chapter 4. Then obtain a copy of page 25 to gain a better understanding of this frustrating situation.

9. Language Arts

In chapter 9, Papa teaches Cassie a very important lesson about life when he compares their lives to that of a fig tree. Writers often use *analogies,* or comparisons, to explain things that might be hard to understand. Reread the paragraph with the fig tree analogy and study it. Did Papa's analogy make it easier for Cassie to understand what he was trying to teach her? Obtain a copy of page 26 from your teacher to complete as directed.

10. Art

Jeremy likes to be up in the trees where it is cool and quiet. He feels like he is in another world when he is up in the tree house he built. Research tree houses. Then design a tree house that you would like to have as your special place. Use craft sticks or cereal boxes to make a model of your tree house. Include furniture and other objects you would like to have. Title your model; then display it in the classroom.

11. Science

A fire in the cotton fields would be devastating to farmers and sharecroppers alike. Papa and Mr. Morrison know that this kind of threat is the only thing that can stop the lynch mob from hurting or even killing T. J. Reread chapter 12 and make a list of the methods they used to fight the fire. Then research modern fire fighting and make a list of the methods used today. On poster board, create a Venn diagram showing the similarities and differences between the fire fighting methods used in the book and those of today.

12. Social Studies

The Logan children walk one hour to the Great Faith Elementary and Secondary School because there is no school bus for black children. Reread chapter 1 and record all the facts related to their route from home to school. Then draw a map of the route, using the information provided. Be sure to include a compass showing north, south, east, and west. After the route is drawn, add illustrations to show landmarks along the way.

Signs of Spring

In the book, Cassie notices many things that signal spring is on the way. In the box below, make a list of the words she used to describe what she saw and heard. Then make a list of the words that come to mind when you think about spring. Finally, in the lines provided, use the two lists to write a brief story about the coming of spring.

_____
(Title)

Cassie's Spring

Adjectives   Nouns   Verbs

_____'s Spring

Adjectives   Nouns   Verbs

Note to the teacher: Use with activity #6 on page 22.

What Will Mr. Turner Do?

Mr. Turner is a sharecropper who can barely afford to pay his debts, much less buy anything special for his family. Find out if Mr. Turner will make any money selling his cotton after he pays off his debts to Mr. Montier, his landlord, and his expenses to Mr. Wallace, the store owner, by answering the questions at the bottom of the page.

Wallace's General Store
Bill of Sale
Autumn

	$15.00
Fertilizer	$10.00
Food	$10.00
Clothing/Misc.	

Wallace's General Store
Bill of Sale
Spring

Tools	$40.00
Mule	$30.00
Seed	$20.00
Fertilizer	$15.00
Food	$10.00
Clothing/Misc.	$10.00

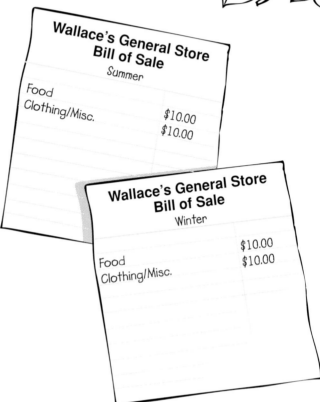

Wallace's General Store
Bill of Sale
Summer

Food	
Clothing/Misc.	$10.00
	$10.00

Wallace's General Store
Bill of Sale
Winter

	$10.00
Food	$10.00
Clothing/Misc.	

1. What was the total amount of money Mr. Turner spent at Wallace's store for the year?

   _____

2. If Mr. Wallace charges 10% interest, how much more would Mr. Turner owe? (Divide the total amount from #1 by 10.) _____

3. If the cotton crop sold for $400.00 and Mr. Montier kept one-half of the money as his portion of the profits, how much would he keep? _____

4. If Mr. Montier charged an additional 10% on that $400.00 as risk money, how much more would he take? _____

5. If you add up all of Mr. Turner's expenses and debts, how much money would he owe? (Add the totals from #1 to 4.) _____

6. Can Mr. Turner pay all of his expenses? If not, how much more does he owe? _____

   _____

7. What can Mr. Turner do about this? _____

   _____

Fig Tree to Family

Papa compares his family to a fig tree. He wants to help Cassie understand that just as roots are important to a fig tree's survival, family roots are important to a family's survival.

I. Directions: Read each analogy below. (Remember, an *analogy* shows a likeness between two objects that are otherwise unlike.) Think about how the words in the first pair go together; then choose a word from the list that completes the second pair. Write the word in the blank.

1. *Branch* is to *tree* as *arm* is to __ __ __ __. `13`

2. *Cotton* is to *cloth* as *peanuts* are to __ __ __ __ __ __ __ __ __ __ __. `12` `10`

3. *Courtroom* is to *lawyer* as __ __ __ __ __ __ __ __ __ is to *teacher*. `8`

4. *Fire* is to *cotton* as *losing the land* is to the __ __ __ __ __ __. `6`

5. *Dog* is to *puppy* as __ __ __ __ __ is to *gosling*. `1`

6. *Roots* are to a *fig tree* as *Big Ma* and *Uncle Hammer* are to __ __ __ __ __ __ __. `4`

7. *Mosquito* is to *fly* as *duck* is to __ __ __ __ __ __. `7`

8. *Papa* is to *Uncle Hammer* as __ __ __ __ __ __ __ __ __ is to *Stacey*. `2` `14`

9. *Sweet potato* is to *vegetable* as __ __ __ __ __ __ __ __ __ __ is to *fruit*. `11` `9`

10. *Serf* is to *king* as __ __ __ __ __ __ __ __ __ __ __ __ is to *landlord*. `5` `3`

Word List

watermelon	waddle	sharecropper	body	classroom
goose	Cassie	peanut butter	Little Man	Logans

II. Directions: Match a circled letter to each numbered blank below to answer the following riddle: What is the name of the smartest cookie in the world?

The __ __ __ __ __ __ __ __ "Fig" __ __ __ __ __ __ !
    1 2 3   4 5 6 7 8   9 10 11 12 13 14

Bonus Box: On the back of this sheet write three analogies of your own using the ones above as a guide.

Name_____

Write a s

1. Be al

2. Early

3. One t

4. Speak

5. Well o

Write your

6. You m

7. No gai

8. When

9. Look a

10. Don't t

Write one m

Ben and Me
by Robert Lawson

About the Book

The life of Benjamin Franklin, one of the most important men in colonial times, is recorded in *Ben and Me* by his close friend and associate Amos the mouse. Author Robert Lawson claims to have been given Amos's tiny journals in which Amos boasts of being the wisdom behind this famous man. Amos, under the cover of Ben's fur hat, influences Ben's writing, experiments, and political activities. Their relationship is based on a written contract which states that Amos will advise Ben in exchange for a home, food, clothing, protection, and the care of his large family. With this agreement, Ben and Amos become lifelong companions.

About the Author

Robert Lawson is the only author who has received both the prestigious Newbery and Caldecott Medals. He was born in New York City in 1892 and grew up in New Jersey. As a child he was an avid reader and greatly admired famous illustrators. He attended the New York School of Fine and Applied Arts and then established himself as an illustrator for several magazines. In 1922 he married fellow illustrator Marie Abrams and they supported themselves by designing greeting cards for years. In 1930 he illustrated his first book, *The Wee Men of Ballywooden* by Arthur Mason. Later, he was asked by a publisher to suggest a subject of his interest to illustrate. When he came up with the idea for *Ben and Me,* the publisher asked him to write the book. Lawson won many awards and honors during his career. He died at his home, Rabbit Hill, in 1957.

Student Contract Materials List

- Activity #1: copy of page 30, construction paper, glue
- Activity #2: four 8½" x 11" sheets of paper; reference materials on friends of Ben Franklin, including George Washington and Thomas Jefferson; crayons or markers; stapler
- Activity #3: copy of page 31
- Activity #4: reference materials on Ben Franklin, crayons or markers
- Activity #5: reference books, magazines, poster board, glue, crayons or markers
- Activity #6: colonial cookbook, white paper
- Activity #7: copy of page 32
- Activity #8: paper
- Activity #9: tape recorder, blank tape, instrumental music
- Activity #10: reference materials, world map
- Activity #11: reference materials on the Declaration of Independence
- Activity #12: science books, battery, insulated wire, iron bolt, crayons or markers

Name _____

Telling Tides

Use the Tide Table to answer the questions below.

1. On the 10th, when was the first low tide? _____

2. On the 10th, when was the first high tide? _____

3. On the 10th, about how many hours passed between low tide and high tide? _____

4. On the 18th, when was the second low tide? _____

5. On the 18th, when was the second high tide? _____

6. On the 18th, about how many hours passed between low tide and high tide? _____

7. On the 20th, when was the first low tide? _____

8. On the 20th, when was the first high tide? _____

9. On the 20th, how many hours passed between low tide and high tide? _____

10. If a shipmaster wanted to sail during high tide between 7:00 A.M. and 8:00 A.M., which days would he choose?

    _____

11. If a shipmaster wanted to dock during high tide between 5:00 P.M. and 7:00 P.M., which days would he choose?

    _____

12. What day has the earliest low tide? _____ Latest low tide? _____

Date	Low 1	Low 2	High 1	High 2
1	12:31 P.M.		5:54 A.M.	6:28 P.M.
2	12:37 A.M.	1:17 P.M.	6:39 A.M.	7:09 P.M.
3	1:22 A.M.	1:58 P.M.	7:19 A.M.	7:48 P.M.
4	2:05 A.M.	2:38 P.M.	7:58 A.M.	8:25 P.M.
5	2:47 A.M.	3:17 P.M.	8:37 A.M.	9:01 P.M.
6	3:29 A.M.	3:56 P.M.	9:16 A.M.	9:38 P.M.
7	4:12 A.M.	4:35 P.M.	9:56 A.M.	10:17 P.M.
8	4:57 A.M.	5:15 P.M.	10:37 A.M.	10:58 P.M.
9	5:44 A.M.	5:59 P.M.	11:22 A.M.	11:43 P.M.
10	6:37 A.M.	6:46 P.M.	12:11 P.M.	
11	7:33 A.M.	7:40 P.M.	12:34 A.M.	1:05 P.M.
12	8:34 A.M.	8:41 P.M.	1:31 A.M.	2:08 P.M.
13	9:37 A.M.	9:45 P.M.	2:35 A.M.	3:17 P.M.
14	10:40 A.M.	10:50 P.M.	3:43 A.M.	4:27 P.M.
15	11:39 A.M.	11:51 P.M.	4:51 A.M.	5:32 P.M.
16	12:34 P.M.		5:55 A.M.	6:31 P.M.
17	12:47 A.M.	1:26 P.M.	6:53 A.M.	7:23 P.M.
18	1:41 A.M.	2:14 P.M.	7:46 A.M.	8:11 P.M.
19	2:32 A.M.	3:00 P.M.	8:35 A.M.	8:57 P.M.
20	3:21 A.M.	3:44 P.M.	9:21 A.M.	9:40 P.M.

Pedro's Journal
by Pam Conrad

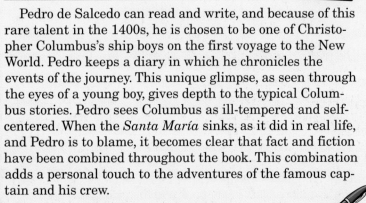

About the Book

Pedro de Salcedo can read and write, and because of this rare talent in the 1400s, he is chosen to be one of Christopher Columbus's ship boys on the first voyage to the New World. Pedro keeps a diary in which he chronicles the events of the journey. This unique glimpse, as seen through the eyes of a young boy, gives depth to the typical Columbus stories. Pedro sees Columbus as ill-tempered and self-centered. When the *Santa María* sinks, as it did in real life, and Pedro is to blame, it becomes clear that fact and fiction have been combined throughout the book. This combination adds a personal touch to the adventures of the famous captain and his crew.

About the Author

Pam Conrad was born in New York on June 18, 1947. Conrad loved writing from the age of seven, when she stayed home with the chicken pox. Instead of drawing with the colored pencils and paper her mother gave her, she began writing poetry. She even entered a writing contest when she was in the fourth grade and won a beagle puppy!

Conrad attended Hofstra University, and eventually received her bachelor's degree from New School for Social Research. When she started writing books and sending them to publishers, she would keep the rejection slips on her desktop spike. By the time she sold her first book, she had 222 rejection slips.

Conrad wrote both picture and young adult books. One of her more popular books, *Prairie Songs,* won the International Reading Association Children's Book Award as well as several other awards. Conrad said that although her books were not entirely based on her own life, parts of her life are in each one. The books she wrote for younger children are based on the lives of her daughters, Johanna and Sarah. Conrad lived on Long Island, New York, until her death in 1996.

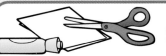

Student Contract Materials List

- Activity #1: white paper, dictionary
- Activity #2: copy of page 36
- Activity #3: reference materials on coral reefs, shoebox, arts-and-crafts supplies, glue, scissors
- Activity #4: paper, pencil
- Activity #5: reference materials on early explorers, world map, colored pencils
- Activity #6: 3 empty soup cans, masking tape, 2 pencils
- Activity #7: white paper, colored pencils or markers
- Activity #8: 1 sheet of 12" x 18" white construction paper, crayons or markers
- Activity #9: reference materials on compasses, magnet, needle, piece of cork, bowl of water
- Activity #10: 2 empty 8-oz. water bottles, 6 oz. sand, balloon, rubber band, duct tape, sharpened pencil
- Activity #11: copy of page 37
- Activity #12: copy of page 38

Pedro's Journal
Independent Contract

Name:_____ Number of activities to be completed: _____

Language Arts
1.

Pedro is assigned to Christopher Columbus's crew, not because he is an experienced sailor, but because he can read and write. Pedro learns about the ship as he goes along. There are many special words that sailors use. Find the meaning of each of these terms as they relate to ships: *fore-and-aft, stern, spar, rudder, boatswain, helm, fathoms, tiller, mutiny, gunwale, mainmast, poop, anchor, sandglass,* and *mast.* Find five additional words used by sailors in the book and then look up their definitions. Use all 20 words and definitions to make a dictionary of nautical terms, including illustrations.

Math
2.

On September 18, the captain orders soundings to be taken to measure how deep the ocean is where they are sailing. When their measuring device, which can measure all the way to 200 fathoms, cannot detect the ocean floor, Pedro fears that there is no bottom to the ocean. Obtain a copy of page 36 from your teacher to learn about fathoms and the depths of the ocean.

Science
3.

On December 25, the *Santa María* sinks off the coast of Punta Santa. Pedro records that he was steering the ship at the time and did not recognize the warning sounds. The real *Santa María* actually did sink after running into a coral reef. Research coral reefs to find out what they are and how they are formed. Then create a diorama of a coral reef.

Language Arts
4.

The ships take on fresh supplies on September 3. No one knows how long they will be at sea, so they stock up with food that will not spoil. In Pedro's record of the supplies, he mentions molasses, dried meat, and salted fish. Imagine that you are responsible for planning the meals for a long trip at sea. Go to your local grocery store and make a list of items that you could take with you that would not spoil on a long voyage. Then create a menu for one week, including breakfasts, lunches, and dinners.

Social Studies
5.

Pedro refers to the voyage that Marco Polo made before Columbus's journey. Research Marco Polo, Amerigo Vespucci, and Vasco da Gama. Find out what they were searching for, what trade routes they followed, and what they found. Then, on a copy of a world map, show each explorer's route(s) in a different color. On the route line of each explorer, write what that explorer is credited with doing or discovering.

Music
6.

Many tourists today visit the Bahamas, which Columbus discovered in 1492. If you visited one of these islands, you would likely hear calypso music played by a steel drum band. Learn about the history of steel drums and calypso music. Next, make three steel drums from different-sized soup cans. Empty the cans and wash them thoroughly. Put masking tape around the edges of the opened end for safety. Then use two eraser-topped pencils to play your steel drums!

Pedro's Journal
Independent Contract

Name: _____ Number of activities to be completed: _____

7. Writing

On October 8, Sancho lets Pedro steer the ship, and Pedro begins to imagine that he is the captain of the newly discovered seas, returning home with his ship laden with riches. Reread this journal entry and then imagine that you are the captain returning home from an incredible adventure at sea. Think about the story you would tell. Then write and illustrate a comic strip telling and showing the amazing things you saw and did.

8. Art

On October 12, when the sailors finally reach land, Christopher Columbus jumps out of the boat first and plants a royal banner in the sand. This banner is in honor of the king and queen, and is meant to claim the land for Spain. Imagine that you have just discovered a new land. Design a banner using colors, words, and symbols that are meaningful to you. On the back of the banner, create a key explaining what each color and symbol represents.

9. Social Studies

On September 13, Pedro describes a navigational problem that the crew is very worried about. Reread this entry to find out what worried the crew. Research early compasses. Next, refer to the information you find to make a simple compass using a magnet, a needle, a piece of cork board, and a bowl of water. Make sure your compass points north. Then demonstrate and explain how your compass works to the class.

10. Science

One of Pedro's duties is to turn the sandglass and call out the time at the exact moment it empties. Follow these directions to make your own sandglass. Fill one eight-ounce bottle three-fourths full of sand. Stretch a balloon over the opening of the bottle and secure it with a rubber band. Using a sharpened pencil, carefully poke a hole in the center of the balloon. Then turn another eight-ounce bottle over on top of the sand-filled bottle and tape the two bottles together using duct tape. Turn the sandglass over and record the amount of time it takes the sand to empty into the other bottle. This is your sandglass time.

11. Math

On September 10, Pedro writes that the crew starts to panic, so the Captain promises them all sorts of riches and fame. Christopher Columbus says he will give a reward of 10,000 *maravedis* to the first man to spot land. Obtain a copy of page 37 from your teacher to discover the value of maravedis.

12. Social Studies

Columbus's plan is to sail from Palos, Spain, to the Canary Islands off the coast of Africa and then on to India. Obtain a copy of page 38 from your teacher. Then use a world map to help you locate the places important to Columbus.

Can You Fathom That?

A *fathom* is equal to six feet and is used to measure the depth of water.
Use this information to answer each question below.

1. Christopher Columbus crossed the Atlantic Ocean, which has an average depth of 14,000 feet (the same as the Pacific Ocean). About how many fathoms would that equal?

   _____

2. Columbus's men could measure as far down as 200 fathoms. How many feet would that equal? _____

3. How many fathoms was Columbus from reaching the bottom of the ocean, assuming that they were at the average depth? _____

4. The deepest known spot in the Atlantic Ocean is the Puerto Rico Trench, which is 28,374 feet deep. How many fathoms would that equal? _____

5. The deepest known spot in the world is the Mariana Trench in the Pacific Ocean. It is 36,198 feet deep. About how many fathoms deeper is the trench than the average depth of the Pacific Ocean? _____

6. The Indian Ocean's average depth is 13,000 feet. About how many fathoms would that equal? _____

7. The deepest known spot in the Indian Ocean is 25,344 feet deep. About how many fathoms deeper is the Puerto Rico Trench than the deepest point in the Indian Ocean? _____

8. The Arctic Ocean's average depth is 4,362 feet. About how many fathoms deeper is the Atlantic Ocean? _____

9. The deepest known spot in the Arctic Ocean is 17,880 feet deep. How many fathoms would that equal? _____

10. Complete the graph by shading the average depths and the deepest points of each ocean.

Fathoms								
7,000								
6,000								
5,000								
4,000								
3,000								
2,000								
1,000								
0	Average	Deepest	Average	Deepest	Average	Deepest	Average	Deepest
	Atlantic Ocean		Pacific Ocean		Indian Ocean		Arctic Ocean	

©2000 The Education Center, Inc. • *Contracts for Independent Readers* • Historical Fiction • TEC792 Key p. 63

Maravedis to Dollars

Compare maravedis and dollars to discover how much Columbus promised to the first person who saw land. Keep in mind that in Columbus's day everything cost much less than it does today, so when Columbus promised 10,000 maravedis, that was a lot of money!

about 7,000 maravedis = about $1.00

The price of each item is given below. Find the total cost of each group of items in dollars and maravedis. The first one is done for you.

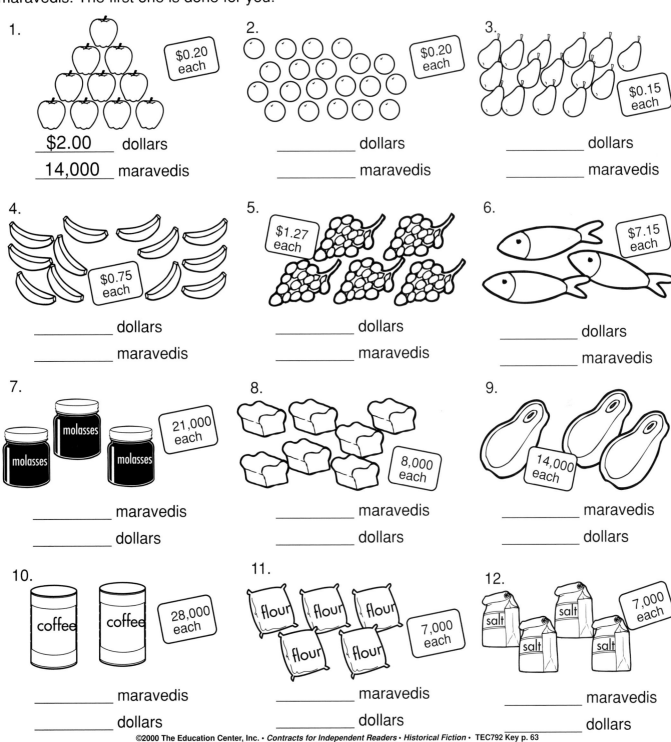

1.
$0.20
each

$2.00 dollars
14,000 maravedis

2.
$0.20
each

_____ dollars
_____ maravedis

3.
$0.15
each

_____ dollars
_____ maravedis

4.
$0.75
each

_____ dollars
_____ maravedis

5.
$1.27
each

_____ dollars
_____ maravedis

6.
$7.15
each

_____ dollars
_____ maravedis

7.
molasses
molasses
molasses
21,000
each

_____ maravedis
_____ dollars

8.
8,000
each

_____ maravedis
_____ dollars

9.
14,000
each

_____ maravedis
_____ dollars

10.
coffee
coffee
28,000
each

_____ maravedis
_____ dollars

11.
flour flour flour
flour flour
7,000
each

_____ maravedis
_____ dollars

12.
salt salt
salt salt
7,000
each

_____ maravedis
_____ dollars

Where Was Columbus Going?

Answer the questions at the bottom of the page by using the map below to discover where Columbus wanted to go and where he actually went.

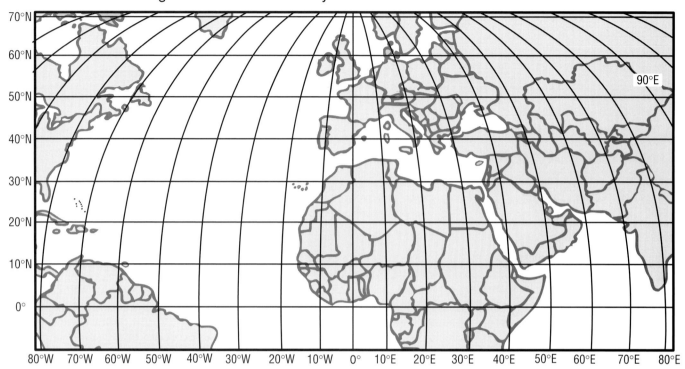

1. Use reference materials to find each of the following locations. Then, on the map above, label and highlight each one in a different color.

   Spain   Canary Islands   Bahamas   India

2. What lines of latitude are each of the following locations between? Record them in the spaces provided.
   Canary Islands _____
   Bahamas _____
   India _____

3. Are the Bahamas at the same latitude as any part of India? _____

4. What lines of longitude are each of the following locations between? Record them in the spaces provided.
   Canary Islands _____
   Bahamas _____
   India _____

5. Are the Bahamas at the same longitude as any part of India? _____

6. If Columbus had known the latitudes and longitudes of India, would he have thought that he was in India when he landed in the Bahamas? _____
   What do you think he would have done differently when he reached the Bahamas if he had known he was not in India? _____
   _____
   _____

©2000 The Education Center, Inc. • *Contracts for Independent Readers • Historical Fiction* • TEC792 Key p. 63

38   **Note to the teacher:** Use with activity #12 on page 35.

The True Confessions of Charlotte Doyle

by Avi

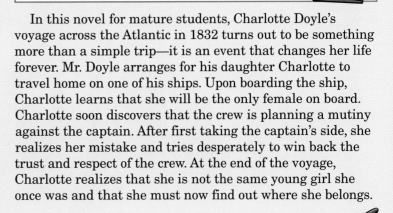

About the Book

In this novel for mature students, Charlotte Doyle's voyage across the Atlantic in 1832 turns out to be something more than a simple trip—it is an event that changes her life forever. Mr. Doyle arranges for his daughter Charlotte to travel home on one of his ships. Upon boarding the ship, Charlotte learns that she will be the only female on board. Charlotte soon discovers that the crew is planning a mutiny against the captain. After first taking the captain's side, she realizes her mistake and tries desperately to win back the trust and respect of the crew. At the end of the voyage, Charlotte realizes that she is not the same young girl she once was and that she must now find out where she belongs.

About the Author

Born on December 23, 1937, Avi was raised with his brother and twin sister in Brooklyn, New York. His name was given to him by his sister when they were one year old, and it stuck. Avi was not a strong student. After he almost flunked out of high school, his parents enrolled him in a small private school that focused on reading and writing. Here, his English teacher insisted he go to a tutor or fail the course. Avi spent the summer learning how to write and learning to want to write.

Avi graduated from the University of Wisconsin and received a master's degree in library science from Columbia University in 1964. He has worked for many years as a librarian and teaches college courses in children's literature. Avi did not set out to write children's books. His first book, *Things That Sometimes Happen,* came out of a game that he played with his sons. Avi learned that he loved to write for children, that he was good at it, and that the response from his readers was his reward. However, writing still doesn't come easily to Avi. It takes him about a year to write one book.

Student Contract Materials List

- Activity #1: copy of page 42
- Activity #2: poster board, white construction paper, crayons or markers, scissors
- Activity #3: world map
- Activity #4: paper, pencil
- Activity #5: 1 sheet of 12" x 18" light-colored construction paper
- Activity #6: $\frac{1}{8}$ tsp. baking soda, 1 c. flour, $\frac{3}{8}$ tsp. salt, 3 tbsp. buttermilk, 4 tsp. maple syrup, $1\frac{1}{2}$ tbsp. shortening

- Activity #7: copy of page 43
- Activity #8: tall tales
- Activity #9: copy of page 44
- Activity #10: masking tape, tape measure
- Activity #11: reference materials on hurricanes, hurricane tracking map, construction paper
- Activity #12: reference materials on mutiny and round robins

The True Confessions of Charlotte Doyle

Independent Contract

Name:_____ Number of activities to be completed: _____

1. Language Arts

Charlotte is first introduced to many of the crewmen in chapter 3 when they assemble before the captain. In all of Charlotte's proper and refined life, she has never seen such a sorry-looking group of men. At this point in the story the crew is little more than a group of names, but as the story develops so does her relationship with each of them. Obtain a copy of page 42 from your teacher and complete it as directed to test your knowledge of the crew.

2. Art

When Charlotte begins her voyage, she has proper lady's attire. Her clothing, complete with dresses, shoes, and gloves, is neatly wrapped in tissue paper in her trunk. Later, when she wants to prove her resolve to join the crew, she changes into a pair of trousers and a blouse. Design and cut out a poster board model of Charlotte, and then illustrate and cut out several outfits for her to wear. Use the cutouts to act out the scene where she decides to become one of the crew, or one of your favorite scenes.

3. Math

The voyage from England to Rhode Island during Charlotte's time period typically took one to two months. Look on a map and determine the distance between these two places. Figure out how many miles per day they would need to travel to get to Providence in one month and then two months. Skim through the book to find out the exact date the *Seahawk* set sail and when it arrived in Providence. How many days was this? Use this information to find the average number of miles they traveled each day. Compare this with how fast the average automobile can travel per hour!

4. Social Studies

Charlotte's life aboard the *Seahawk* is quite boring until she becomes a member of the crew. Then she shares all the chores and responsibilities with the rest of the crewmen. Reread the first few pages of chapter 14. Then make a list of the chores Charlotte is required to do. Choose five of the chores to act out and explain to your classmates.

5. Art

In chapter 1 Charlotte asks about the type of ship the *Seahawk* is. She is told it is a brig, or two-masted ship. Study the diagrams provided in the appendix of the book. Then, on construction paper, draw and label a diagram of the *Seahawk*. Show the crew, the captain, and Charlotte aboard the ship.

6. Science

On the ship Charlotte eats *hardtack,* or sailor's bread. Follow the recipe below to make a batch of hardtack.

1. Mix together $\frac{1}{8}$ teaspon baking soda, 1 cup flour, and $\frac{3}{8}$ teaspoon salt. Then use a fork to mix in 3 tablespoons buttermilk, 4 teaspoons maple syrup, and $1\frac{1}{2}$ tablespoons shortening. Knead the mixture to make dough.
2. Use a rolling pin to roll the dough very thin. Then put the dough on a lightly greased cookie sheet, cut it into squares, and poke holes in it using a fork.
3. With adult supervision, bake the dough at 425° for about 15 minutes or until golden brown. Let it cool before serving.

©2000 The Education Center, Inc. • *Contracts for Independent Readers • Historical Fiction •* TEC792

The True Confessions of Charlotte Doyle

Independent Contract

Name:_____   Number of activities to be completed: _____

7. Language Arts

"Chaos on shipboard is sailing without a rudder." These words of wisdom are typical of the captain, who speaks them on the first day he invites Charlotte to tea in his cabin. The rudder is what steers the ship. The captain uses this metaphor to compare the image of a ship sailing out of control to a crew that is out of control. Obtain a copy of page 43 from your teacher and complete it as directed to match each sailor with his quote.

8. Writing

The crew members of the *Seahawk* entertain one another with *yarns,* or tall tales, of life at sea. When it comes to their yarns, Charlotte isn't always sure what is true and what isn't. Read some tall tales to see how a simple story can be stretched to create a yarn. Use your imagination to write your own yarn about the sea. Try to impress your classmates with your tale, just as the sailors tried to impress each other.

9. Math

The sailors have a specialized vocabulary that includes words pertaining to things of the sea and sailing. Their way of telling time is based on time periods called *watches.* To keep track of the time, a series of bells ring. Sailors don't talk about the time of day by the hour, but rather by the watch or the bells. Obtain a copy of page 44 from your teacher to practice telling time the nautical way.

10. Math

Charlotte gasps at the sight of the cabin to which she is assigned. It is small and dark, measuring 6 feet long, 4 feet wide, and $4\frac{1}{2}$ feet high. Estimate how many of your classmates could fit into the room. Then estimate your classmates' heights and make a list of the classmates who could stand up straight in the cabin. Tape the measurements of the cabin on the floor in front of a chalkboard. Draw a line on the chalkboard showing where the $4\frac{1}{2}$-foot ceiling would be. With your classmates' help, check your estimates.

11. Science

The crew of the *Seahawk* is put to the test when they encounter a hurricane. The ferocity of the storm—with its thunder, lightning, winds, and rain—makes it almost impossible for the crew members to hear each other. The violent movement of the ship makes every step a major struggle. Research hurricanes to find out how they are formed, how they are categorized, what to do if caught in one, and any other interesting information. Then present your research in a weather report with maps showing where most hurricanes develop.

12. Research

Charlotte goes to Captain Jaggery with the report that she saw the document he had warned her about, a *round robin,* or pact among the crew to commit mutiny. When Charlotte discovers a round robin does exist, her whole life changes. Find the definition for mutiny and round robin in the dictionary. Then write an article for the *Providence Daily News* about the mutiny on the *Seahawk.* Make sure your article answers who, what, when, where, why, and how.

Name _____

42

Who's Who of the Crew?

Think about the types of things each of the crew members would say or do. Who says mean things? Who tries to help others? Then match each crew member's name to the description that best fits him.

_____ 1. Barlow

_____ 2. Cranick

_____ 3. Ewing

_____ 4. Fisk

_____ 5. Foley

_____ 6. Grimes

_____ 7. Hollybrass

_____ 8. Jaggery

_____ 9. Johnson

_____ 10. Keetch

_____ 11. Morgan

_____ 12. Zachariah

a. He suggests in chapter 13 that Charlotte climb up to the royal yard to prove her willingness to serve as a fellow crewman.

b. This crewman barely speaks at all until chapter 12.

c. In chapter 2, this decrepit old sailor brings Charlotte her trunk and warns her not to stay on board.

d. This sailor tells Charlotte in chapter 14 that she is the cause of the captain's every move.

e. He is introduced in chapter 9 as a young, handsome, blond Scotsman.

f. In chapter 12, this crewman takes over Zachariah's duties in the galley.

g. He is the only crewman who doesn't sign the round robin. He is then appointed second mate when Keetch is demoted in chapter 12.

h. In chapter 2, this sailor introduces himself as the ship's cook, surgeon, carpenter, and preacher.

i. This first mate is murdered during the hurricane in chapter 15.

j. In chapter 21, it is discovered that this second mate remains faithful to the captain.

k. This stowaway leads the mutiny and is murdered by the captain in chapter 10.

l. In chapters 11 and 12, Charlotte discovers how ruthless and powerful this ship's leader really is.

Note to the teacher: Use with activity #1 on page 40.

Name _____

 # A Quandary of Quotes

The words of the crew have gotten all mixed up! Some of the letters in the words below have been replaced with symbols and numerals. As you figure out each letter, write it next to its symbol or numeral in the treasure chest below. Next, use the treasure chest to rewrite each quote, replacing the missing letters. Then write what you think the crewman is trying to say. The first one is done for you.

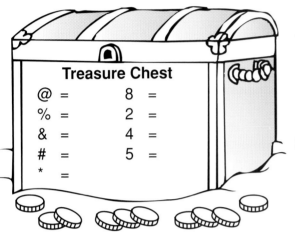

Treasure Chest

@ =		8 =	
% =		2 =	
& =		4 =	
# =		5 =	
* =			

1. "&@# 5lw5y8 @##28 5 %i@5l %ri#@2," says Zachariah in chapter 2. *"One always needs a final friend." When a sailor dies, he needs a friend to sew him into his hammock and throw his body overboard.*

2. In chapter 8 Captain Jaggery says, "I 8h5ll *r#5k 4h#m 4& my will." _____

    _____

3. "*#w5r# y&ur %ri#@2, Mi88 2&yl#, *#w5r# him," warns Mr. Fisk in chapter 12. _____

    _____

    _____

4. In chapter 10 Zachariah states, "58 5 m5@ h# cl5im8 &ur m#rcy." _____

    _____

    _____

5. "@& &@# r5@k8 %&r cr#54iv# g#@iu8 lik# 5 85il&r 8hirki@g w&rk," snarls Captain Jaggery in chapter 8. _____

    _____

    _____

6. In chapter 13 Ewing tells Charlotte, "K##p y&ur #y#8 84#52y &@ 4h# r&p#8. 2&@'4 y&u l&&k 2&w@. &r up." _____

    _____

    _____

7. "&@# 8hipm54# h#lp8 5@&4h#r," Zachariah states in chapter 17. _____

    _____

    _____

8. Captain Jaggery says, "8w##4 5r# 4h# u8#8 &% 52v#r8i4y" in chapter 8. _____

    _____

    _____

Note to the teacher: Use with activity #7 on page 41.

The True Confessions of Charlotte Doyle

Mind Your Watch

I. Use the ships' time chart below to identify the times listed. Write the actual time in the space provided.

Ships' Time Chart

midwatch	= 12:00 A.M. (midnight)–4:00 A.M.
morning watch	= 4:00 A.M.–8:00 A.M.
forenoon watch	= 8:00 A.M.–12:00 P.M. (noon)
afternoon watch	= 12:00 P.M.(noon)–4:00 P.M.
first dog watch	= 4:00 P.M.–6:00 P.M.
second dog watch	= 6:00 P.M.–8:00 P.M.
night watch	= 8:00 P.M.–12:00 A.M.

1 bell	= the first half hour after the watch begins
2 bells	= the second half hour
3 bells	= the third half hour
4 bells	= the fourth half hour
5 bells	= the fifth half hour
6 bells	= the sixth half hour
7 bells	= the seventh half hour
8 bells	= the eighth half hour and the end of the watch

1. 3 bells after forenoon   _____

2. 8 bells after night watch   _____

3. 2 bells after second dog watch _____

4. 5 bells after morning watch   _____

5. 1 bell after afternoon watch   _____

6. 4 bells after midwatch   _____

II. Use the ships' time chart above to write these hours in ships' time.

7. 2:30 P.M.   _____

8. 8:00 A.M.   _____

9. 5:00 P.M.   _____

10. 3:00 A.M. _____

11. 11:30 P.M. _____

12. 5:30 A.M. _____

©2000 The Education Center, Inc. • *Contracts for Independent Readers* • *Historical Fiction* • TEC792 • Key p. 64

Note to the teacher: Use with activity #9 on page 41.

Dragonwings

by Laurence Yep

About the Book

For eight years, Moon Shadow has lived with his mother, while the father he has never met lives in the Land of the Golden Mountain. But now it is time for Moon Shadow to cross the ocean and live with his father, Windrider. Windrider dreams of flying, and soon Moon Shadow shares his dream. They spend their spare time working side by side studying books and building model planes until they finally build their plane, *Dragonwings*. Windrider takes *Dragonwings* out for its first and only flight in 1909. Having fulfilled one dream, Windrider begins pursuing a new dream—to reunite his family.

About the Author

Laurence Yep, a third-generation Chinese-American, was born in San Francisco, California, on June 14, 1948. He lived in the West End, but attended school in San Francisco's Chinatown, where he felt like an outsider because he did not speak Chinese. When he played war with friends, he was the Japanese who got killed or the North Korean Communist. Having no particular culture contributed to Yep's overall feeling of alienation. These feelings were to become a central theme on which his later writings were based. He began writing science fiction in high school and had his first story accepted at the age of 18. He later realized that he always placed his characters in a dual setting, like China and America, so he began concentrating on this theme.

Yep graduated from the University of California at Santa Cruz and by 1975, had earned his Ph.D. in English from the State University of New York at Buffalo. He has been a part-time instructor of English, a visiting lecturer in Asian-American Studies, and has received many awards for his outstanding work. *Dragonwings* alone won nine awards!

Student Contract Materials List

- Activity #1: paper, pencil
- Activity #2: white drawing paper
- Activity #3: copy of page 48, 1 sheet of 12" x 18" light-colored construction paper, scissors, glue
- Activity #4: reference materials on the Chinese New Year
- Activity #5: copy of page 49
- Activity #6: reference materials on kites; building materials, such as straws, string, dowel rods, and tissue and construction paper
- Activity #7: reference materials on the Chinese language, 1 sheet of 12" x 18" light-colored construction paper, crayons or markers
- Activity #8: white drawing paper, markers or colored pencils
- Activity #9: copy of page 50
- Activity #10: reference materials on constellations, white drawing paper, crayons or markers
- Activity #11: reference materials on the 1906 earthquake, tape recorder, blank tape
- Activity #12: reference materials on games, white drawing paper, markers or crayons

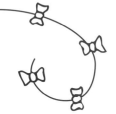

Dragonwings
Independent Contract

Name:_____ Number of activities to be completed: _____

1. Writing

Letters are a vital part of Moon Shadow's life. Before he goes to America, the only contact he has with his father is through letters. After joining his father, he and his mother communicate through letters. Imagine being separated from someone important to you and having to rely on letters to communicate. Write a letter to someone special, telling about your school year. Pretend that this special person has never met the people or seen the things you will be writing about.

2. Art

In chapter 11, Moon Shadow describes the finished *Dragonwings* with such detail that it is easy to picture. Reread this description and sketch the airplane according to Moon Shadow's words. Next, tell your classmates to imagine *Dragonwings* as you read that section of the book to them. Then show them your sketch. Ask your classmates how close your sketch is to what they imagined.

3. Social Studies

Laurence Yep makes many references to real people and actual events in history throughout the book. Obtain a copy of page 48 from your teacher to learn when those events took place.

4. Research

At the beginning of chapter 9, Moon Shadow and Windrider celebrate the Chinese New Year very simply. Research the Chinese New Year. Find out some of the ways Chinese people celebrate this holiday. Then use the following headings to create a chart comparing the typical Chinese New Year and Moon Shadow's New Year: "Foods," "Decorations," "Music," and "Special Customs."

5. Language Arts

Moon Shadow is introduced to many new things that are foreign to him. The way he explains them is very descriptive and amusing. Think about a time when you tried a new food. How would you describe it? Obtain a copy of page 49 from your teacher and complete it as directed to discover what foods Moon Shadow describes.

6. Art

Moon Shadow knows that his father can make the most marvelous kites. When Moon Shadow finally turns eight, he is considered old enough to fly some of his father's special kites. Research kites, their beautiful designs, and their various shapes and sizes. Use the information you find to design your own kite. Then construct a kite of your own, using materials such as straws, dowel rods, tissue paper, string, and construction paper.

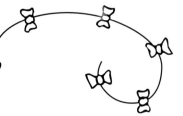

Dragonwings
Independent Contract

Name:_____ Number of activities to be completed: _____

Language Arts

7. Learning a new language is a challenge, and Moon Shadow finds the English language particularly challenging. He thinks a language with only 26 symbols is hard to understand. The Chinese language does not use letters to spell out words, but instead uses pictographs and ideographs to represent objects and ideas. Research written Chinese. Then design a poster with several Chinese pictographs or ideographs, their English translations, and illustrations of their meanings.

Art

8. The Dragon King appears to Windrider in a dream and tells him that in a former life, he was a great flying dragon and that this is where his name came from. Windrider is so impressed by his dream that many years later he repeats it to Moon Shadow. His description of the dream is very detailed. Reread Windrider's description in chapter 3. Based on this description, draw a comic strip of Windrider's dream.

Social Studies

9. There are many new things for Moon Shadow to adjust to in the "demons' land," such as the calendar. He wonders why it isn't like the Chinese calendar. Reread Moon Shadow's comparison of the two calendars in chapter 4. Then obtain a copy of page 50 from your teacher to learn about the Chinese calendar.

Science

10. In chapter 8, Windrider and Moon Shadow talk with Robin and Miss Whitlaw about the constellations. These are the same stars that they saw back in the Middle Kingdom, but here in San Francisco they are called different names and have different stories. Research the three constellations mentioned in the book. Then create an eight-page constellation booklet, containing a front cover, back cover, three pages of drawings of constellations, and three pages of brief descriptions of each constellation.

Science

11. Moon Shadow describes the San Francisco earthquake of 1906 as a nightmare. The earthquake occurs around 5 A.M., so many people are awakened by it. Research the facts about this event. Using what you learned through your research, write an imaginary interview with one of the eyewitnesses. Then record the interview as a friend reads one role and you read the other.

Social Studies

12. Playing games is one way the Tang men spend their free time. In the story, Moon Shadow mentions Mah-Jongg (similar to the card game gin rummy), the Tang people's chess (similar to chess), and jackstraws (similar to pick-up-sticks). Research two of these games. Then make a pamphlet with illustrations explaining the two games you chose.

Once Upon a Timeline

Use the events and dates below to create a timeline of the important events in history mentioned in the story.

Directions: Cut out the events and dates below. On a sheet of construction paper, draw a timeline. Glue each date, in chronological order, onto the timeline. Research each event to find out when it occurred. Then glue the corresponding event next to its date on the timeline.

December 17, 1903	The Wright brothers made the world's first flight in an airplane they invented and built.
1879	Captain Thomas Scott Baldwin flew the *California Arrow*, a motor-driven balloon.
April 18, 1906	E. Nesbit, the author of *The Phoenix and the Carpet*, was born.
August 3, 1904	Theodore Roosevelt became the youngest president of the United States.
August 19, 1858	President William McKinley was shot by an assassin.
September 7, 1901	The Boxer Rebellion was settled, ending the yearlong fighting in China.
August 1876	San Francisco experienced one of the worst earthquakes in the history of the United States.
September 22, 1909	Fung Joe Guey, a young Chinese flier, built and flew his own flying machine.
September 6, 1901	Alexander Graham Bell received the first one-way long distance telephone call.
September 14, 1901	Thomas Alva Edison invented the incandescent lamp.

©2000 The Education Center, Inc. • *Contracts for Independent Readers • Historical Fiction* • TEC792 • Key p. 64

Note to the teacher: Use with activity #3 on page 46.

Name That Food!

I. Read each description below and write the name of the food item in the space provided. Then draw a picture of each item. Hint: The first three food items were mentioned in *Dragonwings*.

1. brown-colored, shaped like men _____	2. thick white liquid with an awful, greasy taste _____	3. thick sandwiches with meat from a fat bird _____
4. thin, yellow, tart, and tangy liquid _____		5. small, round fruits clustered together on skinny branches _____

II. The first three food items listed below are items that Moon Shadow and his father ate in the story. Use the descriptions above to help you write descriptions for these food items. For numbers 9 and 10, name two food items that you like or dislike and write descriptions for them in the spaces provided. Then draw a picture of each item.

6. Chinese tea _____ _____ _____	7. shark's-fin soup _____ _____ _____	8. duck _____ _____ _____
9. _____ _____ _____		10. _____ _____ _____

Note to the teacher: Use with activity #5 on page 46.

 1999   # Comparing Calendars   2000

The Chinese calendar and the calendar used in the United States are based on observations and calculations of astronomers. The two use different methods to mark time in a way that fits the cycles of nature. Both consider day and night and the change of seasons. The Chinese calendar also considers the cycles of the moon. Each calendar uses a pattern with occasional changes to coordinate time with nature. Study the charts below and then answer the questions that follow.

	Chinese Calendar	**Calendar Used by U.S.**
Origin	Legend states 2637 B.C.	45 B.C.
Based on	Lunar and Solar	Solar
Number of Days in a Month (Regular Year)	$29\frac{1}{2}$	28, 30, or 31
Number of Days in a Month (Leap Year)	—	29, 30, or 31
Number of Days in a Regular Year	353, 354, or 355	365
Number of Days in a Leap Year	383, 384, or 385	366
Number of Months in a Regular Year	12	12
Number of Months in a Leap Year	13	—
How Years Are Recorded	Name (Rabbit, Dragon)	Numerically (1999, 2000)
How the New Year Is Determined	New Moon of the First Month	January 1

1. How many days are in a month in the Chinese calendar? _____

2. How many days are in a month in a leap year in the calendar used by the United States? _____

3. How many months are in a Chinese leap year? _____

4. How many months are in a regular year in a calendar used by the United States? _____

5. What is the least number of days in a leap year on the Chinese calendar? _____

6. What is the greatest number of days in a regular year on a calendar used by the United States? _____

7. In the year 2000, about how old was the Chinese calendar? _____

8. In the year 2000, about how old was the calendar used by the United States? _____

Sing Down the Moon
by Scott O'Dell

About the Book

Bright Morning, a 14-year-old Navaho, is happily anticipating all the promises of spring—a rich harvest, shepherding her mother's flock of sheep, and a possible marriage to Tall Boy, the leader of the young warriors. However, none of this will become reality. First, she and her friend Running Bird are kidnapped by Spaniards and sold as slaves. Then Bright Morning and her people are moved from their homes and forced to march to Fort Sumner, where they are imprisoned by the Long Knives. Many die on this historically cruel and tragic Long Walk, and many more die during their imprisonment. Bright Morning fights to get her old life back and raise her son in the way of life to which she was once accustomed.

About the Author

Scott O'Dell was born in Los Angeles, California, on May 23, 1898. His father worked for the railroad, so the family moved often but not very great distances. One home was on Rattlesnake Island, where the water washed up under the stilts that supported their house.

O'Dell attended Occidental College, the University of Wisconsin, and Stanford University. He was not interested in learning all that was required of him. He took the courses that most interested him and did not worry about graduation. After college O'Dell held many jobs, including that of Hollywood cameraman. *Island of the Blue Dolphins* was his first novel for young adults. He claimed that he didn't truly write for children; he wrote for himself, and his experiences come through in his writings. When writing, O'Dell worked every day of the week from 7 A.M. to noon. He received the Newbery Honor award for *Sing Down the Moon*. Scott O'Dell died in 1989.

Student Contract Materials List

- Activity #1: 1 sheet of 12" x 18" light-colored construction paper, crayons or markers
- Activity #2: poster board, string, crayons or markers
- Activity #3: paper, pencil
- Activity #4: copy of page 54
- Activity #5: reference materials on Navahos and Apaches, 1 sheet of 12" x 18" light-colored construction paper, crayons or markers
- Activity #6: reference materials on wild berries, white drawing paper, crayons or markers

- Activity #7: reference materials on weaving, 1 sheet of 12" x 18" white construction paper, crayons or markers
- Activity #8: paper, pencil
- Activity #9: reference materials on hogans; natural materials, such as sticks, clay, and rocks
- Activity #10: copy of page 55, 1 sheet of 12" x 18" construction paper, 3 index cards, glue
- Activity #11: reference materials on The Long Walk, drawing paper, crayons or markers
- Activity #12: Native American music, homemade or authentic instruments

Sing Down the Moon

Independent Contract

Name:_____ Number of activities to be completed: _____

 ### 1. Language Arts

Throughout the book you were introduced to characters in Bright Morning's life whose Native American names are quite different from ones you are probably familiar with, such as Running Bird, Tall Boy, and White Deer. These names were chosen to recognize an accomplishment or to signify something unique about the person. If you could choose your own name, what name would you choose? Write on a sheet of paper your new name, and an explanation of why you selected it. Draw an illustration showing your unique quality or how you earned the name.

 ### 2. Science

Bright Morning spends her days outdoors, so she is very aware of the natural things around her. Bright Morning mentions the eagle, red-tailed hawk, owl, blue jay, and buzzard in the story. Research each bird to find out where it lives, what it eats, and other interesting information. Then create a bird mobile of facts by cutting pieces of poster board into the shapes of the nests, prey, and other information gathered. Write each fact on the back of its corresponding shape.

 ### 3. Writing

A writer can use dialogue to help his readers understand an incident from two sides. Scott O'Dell shows his readers two viewpoints in chapter 17 when Bright Morning's father and mother discuss their feelings about the forced march. Imagine that your family is being forced to move. Write a dialogue between you and a family member about the move. One of you has a positive outlook, and the other has a negative outlook.

 ### 4. Math

Bright Morning uses many ways to mark the passage of time. It was not necessary for the Navahos to measure time by hours and minutes because of the way they lived. Instead they relied on things in nature, such as "when the light shone in the east," to determine the time. Obtain a copy of page 54 from your teacher to discover creative ways to measure time.

 ### 5. Research

In chapter 19 Bright Morning mentions that Apaches were already at Bosque Redondo when they arrived and that they were not happy to see so many Navahos arriving. Research Apaches and Navahos. Then create an illustrated poster comparing the two types of Native Americans. Include the types of dwellings they lived in, weapons they used, food they ate, and any other interesting comparisons you can make.

 ### 6. Language Arts

Wild berries are the first nourishment the people of Bright Morning's village find when they are forced out of their village. Read about edible wild berries that grow in the United States, such as strawberries, blackberries, boysenberries, and raspberries. Then write an advertisement telling all the benefits of eating berries. Include illustrations of berries in various desserts and snacks.

Sing Down the Moon

Independent Contract

Name:_____ Number of activities to be completed: _____

 Art

Bright Morning considers herself a good weaver. Historically, Navaho women have been well-known for their beautifully woven blankets and rugs. Research the history and styles of Navaho blankets. Learn about the different patterns and colors they use and what those patterns and colors signify. Using the information you collect, create your own design. Then write a paragraph explaining what your patterns and colors represent.

 Language Arts

Kin-nadl-dah, the Womanhood Ceremony, was a Navaho tradition that lasted four days. During that time a young girl was asked to perform many tasks to prove she had the qualities important for a woman. Reread chapter 13 and make a list of all the qualities the Navaho admire and respect. Then think of several women whom you admire and respect. What qualities do they have that are admirable? List them alongside Bright Morning's list, and then write why you think Bright Morning's list is important to her people and why your list is important to you.

 Art

Bright Morning and her people live in *hogans*. Research hogans to find out what they look like, what they are made of, and how they are built. Then build a model of a hogan, using natural materials.

 Social Studies

Scott O'Dell uses fictional characters in his book *Sing Down the Moon* to give a firsthand account of The Long Walk, an actual historical event. Obtain a copy of page 55 from your teacher to learn about this event.

 Research

Although Bright Morning is not a real character, the story she tells of The Long Walk is true. Research this tragic episode that took place from 1864 to 1868. Today a memorial is being planned, honoring those who survived The Long Walk. Draw a picture of what you think the memorial should look like. Then write a paragraph explaining why you chose the type of memorial you did.

 Music

Music is very important to Bright Morning and her people. She sings while shepherding her sheep, the medicine man sings 12 songs during Bright Morning's Womanhood Ceremony, and Tall Boy sings a song to his son every night. Research Native American music to find what instruments they use. Then go to the public library and listen to several recordings of Native American music and try to identify the various instruments being played. Gather some homemade or authentic instruments and make up a song patterned after the Native American music you listened to. Play your song for the class.

54 Name _____

What Time Is It?

Instead of using a clock, Bright Morning describes things that occur in nature to tell the time of day. These are things that are familiar to everyone in her village.

I. Read each clock below. For clocks 1–4, write the time of day each description from the book indicates. For example, on page 26 Bright Morning states that she waited for the moon to rise, which would be nighttime. For clocks 5–8, write your own description for each time of day. Use images that would be familiar to your family and friends.

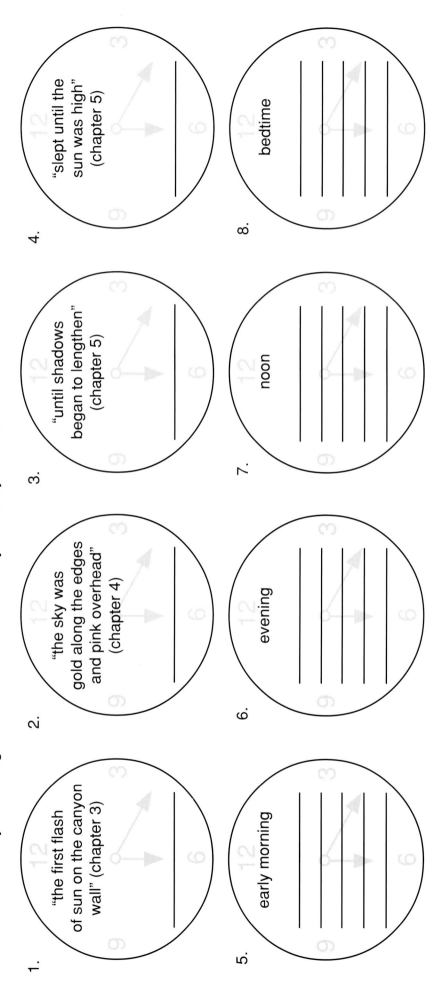

1.

"the first flash of sun on the canyon wall" (chapter 3)

2.

"the sky was gold along the edges and pink overhead" (chapter 4)

3.

"until shadows began to lengthen" (chapter 5)

4.

"slept until the sun was high" (chapter 5)

5.

early morning

6.

evening

7.

noon

8.

bedtime

II. Think of three additional times of the day when you participate in specific activities or events. Write the name of each activity or event and a description of the time it occurs on the back of this sheet.

©2000 The Education Center, Inc. • *Contracts for Independent Readers • Historical Fiction* • TEC792 • Key p. 64

Note to the teacher: Use with Activity #4 on page 52.

The Long Walk

I. Use the map below to answer the questions that follow to learn more about The Long Walk.

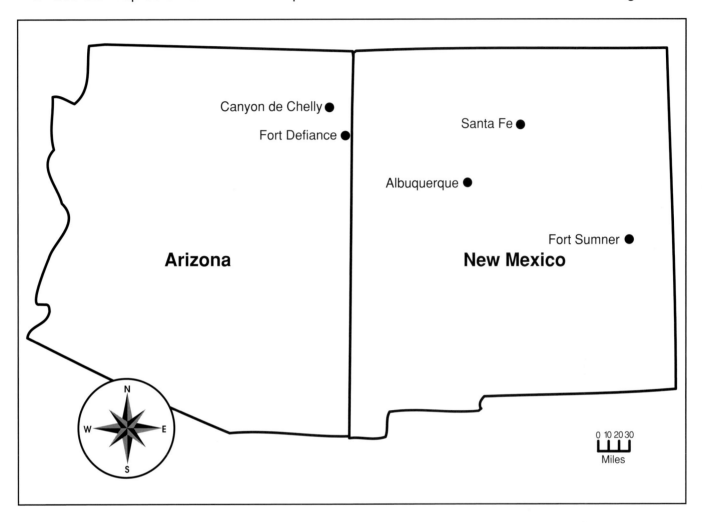

1. On the map, highlight each of these locations: Canyon de Chelly, Arizona; Fort Defiance, Arizona; and Fort Sumner, New Mexico.

2. Draw a path from Canyon de Chelly to Fort Sumner.

3. Soldiers from Fort Defiance came to Canyon de Chelly to force the Navahos off their land. Use the map scale to determine about how many miles Canyon de Chelly is from Fort Defiance. _____

4. About how many miles is Canyon de Chelly from Fort Sumner? _____

5. If it took Bright Morning and her people about 70 days to get to Fort Sumner, about how many miles did they walk each day? _____

II. Glue this page to a sheet of poster board. Label three index cards "Canyon de Chelly," "Fort Defiance," and "Fort Sumner." Write the importance of each location on its corresponding card. Use your book if needed. Then glue the index cards around the map.

Bud, Not Buddy

by Christopher Paul Curtis

About the Book

The Newbery Medal winner for the year 2000 traces the journey of an orphaned boy in the 1930s who perseveres against great odds to find a family. Bud, a ten-year-old black boy, sets off on his own to escape the harsh treatment of foster homes and to find his father. The resourceful Bud has a whole list of rules for "making life funner," which help keep him out of trouble. He also has the courage to open doors that will lead to a better life. His search leads him to Herman E. Calloway, a musician whose publicity flyers his mother saved. To his great surprise, Calloway is not his father, but his grandfather. Among the musicians, Bud finds the family and the love he craves.

About the Author

Christopher Paul Curtis is not your stereotypical writer. He writes his manuscripts in longhand rather than on a computer; his office is a table in the children's section of his local public library rather than a well-equipped desk in a quiet, comfortable room. After high school he worked in a local automotive assembly plant for more than ten years rather than majoring in English in college. Eventually, he pursued his dream of attending college (going part-time while holding down a job) and graduated around the age of 42. His first manuscript was a labor of love by his entire family. At his wife's suggestion, he took a year off from work to write. During that year, she assumed many of the financial responsibilities for the family. Even his son, Steven, helped out by typing his dad's longhand daily writings on the family's computer every night.

Curtis's first novel, *The Watsons Go to Birmingham—1963*, received rave reviews and was awarded many honors, including being selected as a Newbery Honor book. His sister, Cydney, said that this novel was good, but that she felt his best was yet to come. How correct she was. for his second novel, *Bud, Not Buddy,* was the Newbery Medal winner of 2000! This unlikely author, born on May 10, 1954, in Flint, Michigan, has stunned the world of children's literature and is thrilled when children like his books, for he feels that young people are the most honest critics there are.

Student Contract Materials List

- Activity #1: paper, pencil
- Activity #2: tape recorder, instrumental music recording, drawing paper
- Activity #3: paper, pencil
- Activity #4: tape recorder, blank tape, paper
- Activity #5: copy of page 59, 6 index cards
- Activity #6: white construction paper, scissors, black marker, pen
- Activity #7: paper, pencil
- Activity #8: copy of page 60
- Activity #9: Michigan map, highlighter, paper
- Activity #10: reference material on jazz, jazz recording, tape recorder, poster board, markers or crayons, other art materials as desired
- Activity #11: encyclopedias or access to the Internet
- Activity #12: tape player, blank tape

Bud, Not Buddy

Independent Contract

Name:_____ Number of activities to be completed: _____

1. Language Arts

Throughout the book, Bud shares his words of wisdom in his "Rules and Things for Having a Funner Life and Making a Better Liar Out of Yourself." Skim through the book, locate the ten rules Buddy explains, and read them carefully. Select your favorite rule and write it at the top of a sheet of paper. Then write several paragraphs explaining what you think the rule means and why you think Bud chooses to put the rule on his list. Afterward, compose three original rules to share with your classmates.

2. Art

In chapter 17 when Bud first hears Herman E. Calloway and the Dusky Devastators of the Depression rehearse, he is overwhelmed by the power of their music. He visualizes a rainstorm, complete with thunder and lightning. Reread this section; then choose a piece of your favorite instrumental music. Close your eyes as you listen to it and see what images the music conjures up in your mind. Draw a picture that captures the feelings the music evokes, and then bring a recording of the music to class to play as you share your artwork with the class.

3. Writing

Author Christopher Paul Curtis included famous folks from the depression era throughout the book to make the story seem real. Brainstorm a list of people who are famous now. Try to think of people from a diverse range of occupations, such as sports, theater, politics, and science. Write a story set in the state you live in that takes place now. Insert the names of some of these famous people into the story. Be ready to read your story to your classmates and explain who each famous person is.

4. Music

Folk music has strong ties to a place or a culture. It can take a sad or a funny look at life. When Bud and Bugs spend the night in Hooverville, they hear a sad folk song about a man's life on the road. Write a folk song about the place where you live or about your culture. Choose something about the place you live or your culture that makes you feel sad or happy. Then write three sad or funny verses on that topic and put the verses to a tune. Sing your folk song into a tape recorder and play it for the class, or sing it in person!

5. Language Arts

Many of the members of the Herman E. Calloway's Dusky Devastators of the Depression have intriguing nicknames. They take great pride in giving Bud one of his own. Reread the section in chapter 16 where Bud is knighted Sleepy LaBone. How did that name come about? Obtain a copy of page 59 and six index cards from your teacher. Follow the directions to identify some of the nicknames used in the book. Then use your creativity to come up with some nicknames of your own.

6. Social Studies

Bud carries the things that are most important to him in a suitcase. He never lets the suitcase out of his sight. Draw a large suitcase shape on a sheet of construction paper. Cut out the shape. Using a black marker, write a list of at least five things that you could not leave behind if you had to leave your home forever. Beside each thing listed, use a pen to write a sentence explaining why it is so important to you. Tell your parents or other family members about *Bud, Not Buddy.* Then share your suitcase cutout with them.

Bud, Not Buddy
Independent Contract

Name:_____ Number of activities to be completed: _____

7. Math

A telegram was a popular way to send a message before telephones became so easily available and affordable. The message was sent in Morse code over wires. Since you paid by the letter, the sender tried to eliminate all unnecessary words. The word *stop* indicated a period. In chapter 12, you can read the message about Bud that Lefty Lewis sent to Herman E. Calloway. After reviewing the message, write a telegram to a friend describing the book, *Bud, Not Buddy.* You can spend only $1.00. Each letter costs you two cents.

8. Social Studies

All of Bud's worldly possessions are neatly stored in a tattered old suitcase. Among the things that he treasures is a bag of smooth stones. Each stone has a code written on it. Bud does not understand the code, but he keeps the stones because they had been important to his mother. Later, Bud discovers that Herman E. Calloway writes similar codes on stones. This link confirms to both of them that they are related. Obtain a copy of page 60 from your teacher. Write some codes of your own.

9. Social Studies

Bud visits the library to consult an atlas to plan his trip from Flint to Grand Rapids. The distance is about 120 miles. He knows the average man can walk about five miles per hour. He determines it will take him 24 hours to make this trip. Make a copy of a Michigan map. Highlight the cities Flint, Owosso, Ovid, St. John's, Ionia, Lowell, and Grand Rapids. Starting with Flint, compute the time it would take Bud to go from one city to the next. Make a trip timeline of Bud's journey. Mark each city in order on the timeline. In the space between each pair of cities, write the distance traveled and the travel time between the two cities. Display the map and the trip timeline.

10. Music

Bud's grandfather's band is well-known for its incredible jazz music. Research to discover the names of some of the great jazz musicians of all time. Locate a recording by one of those musicians. Listen to the music; then design a poster announcing a gig by that musician to take place in your class. Include a drawing of the musician, a biographical paragraph about the musician, the location and date of the performance, and any other interesting information you feel would make your classmates want to come to the show. Post this in your classroom. On the date specified, play the recording for your class and get everyone tapping their toes to the beat!

11. Social Studies

When the car Bud is riding in is stopped by a police officer, the driver, Lefty Lewis, asks Bud to slide a box beneath his seat. The box contains flyers announcing a meeting of the Brotherhood of Pullman Porters. Lefty explains that the porters are trying to organize a union. Using encyclopedias or researching online, find a few facts about unions during the Great Depression. Select a group that organized a union during that time period and design a flyer announcing a meeting. On the flyer, include what the meeting will be about, where the meeting will take place, the time for the meeting, and a reminder to keep the meeting confidential.

12. Social Studies

Christopher Paul Curtis includes an afterword to his book *Bud, Not Buddy.* In it he explains how he based some of the characters and situations in his book on members of his own family. He regrets that he did not spend more time talking to his grandparents about their lives. Now he realizes that he missed learning from their knowledge, wisdom, and stories. His advice to readers is to talk to parents, grandparents, and other relatives and friends about their lives. Ask an adult relative or friend to tell you some stories from his or her life. Tape the stories to share with your class.

The Name Game

Write the real name of each person whose nickname appears below. In the space provided, write what the nickname Sleepy LaBone means.

1. Steady Eddie _____

2. Thug _____

3. Doo-Doo Bug _____

4. Dirty Deed _____

5. Sleepy LaBone _____

_____

Now it's your turn! Choose six people to nickname. They can be students in your class or famous people whom everyone in your class will know. Make up a positive nickname for each one. Follow the directions below to make a Name Game card for each person. Then follow the directions for playing the Name Game.

To make one card:
1. Fold an index card in half.
2. Write a nickname on the outside as shown and decorate the card.
3. Open the card and write how the nickname was derived on the inside.
4. On the back, write the person's real name in small print.

To play the game:
1. Pair up with a classmate to play the game. Give your classmate one of the cards.
2. First, have your classmate guess who the nickname belongs to without opening the card. If the guess is correct, give your classmate five points. If the guess is incorrect, give yourself five points.
3. Allow your classmate to open the card, read the clue, and guess again. If the guess is correct, give your classmate two points. If the guess is incorrect, give yourself two points and turn over the card to reveal the real name.
4. Continue in the same manner until your classmate has tried to guess all six cards.
5. Count up the points to see who wins!

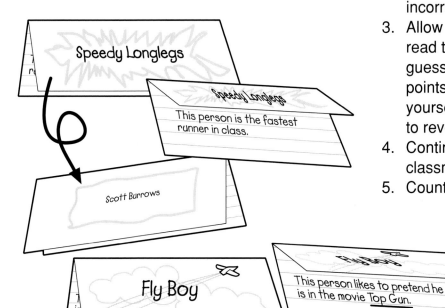

Note to the teacher: Use with activity #5 on page 57.

Messages in Stone

In *Bud, Not Buddy,* Herman E. Calloway writes special codes on smooth stones. Use information from the book to help you decode the messages from the stones described in the story.

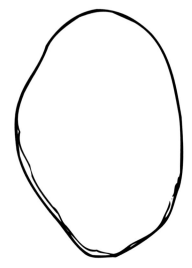

1. kentland ill. 5.10.11 _____

2. loogootee in. 5.16.11 _____

3. sturgis m. 8.30.12 _____

4. gary in. 6.13.12 _____

5. flint m. 8.11.11 _____

6. idlewild m. 5.2.36 _____

7. preston in. 6.4.36 _____

8. chicago il. 3.19.32 _____

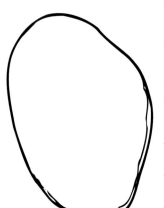

On each of the blank stones around the border, record one important trip or event in your life that you would like to remember. Encode your special memories just as Herman E. Calloway did.

On the lines below, write a brief description of one important trip or event that you have recorded on a stone.

_____

_____

_____

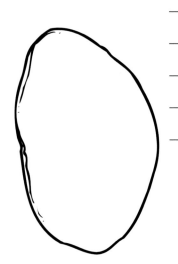

_____

_____

_____

_____

On the High Seas With Historical Fiction

Sail back in time to peruse the prairies, dredge up the Depression,
scour the seas, and stop slavery with this collection of historical fiction novels.

Across the Lines by Carolyn Reeder • Can a friendship survive separation, racial differences, and even war? To find out, read about the lives of Edward and Simon, a boy and his servant who live during the time of the Civil War.

Adaline Falling Star by Mary Pope Osborne • This is the story of Kit Carson's daughter, who leaves a home where she is not wanted to search for her father. What she isn't prepared for is posing as a boy, finding an unusual friend, and working her way across the country!

A Family Apart (The Orphan Train Adventures series) by Joan Lowery Nixon • The orphan train is heading west, and Jennifer and her five brothers and sisters are on it. What will they find in Missouri? Will they be separated? Only time will tell.

The Fighting Ground by Avi • Jonathan thinks that fighting the British will be courageous and exciting. Once involved, however, he finds that fighting is not all that he once believed.

In the Year of the Boar and Jackie Robinson by Bette Bao Lord • What do a boar, a baseball, and a young Chinese girl have in common? Read about Shirley Temple Wong's adventures in a new country to find out!

A Letter to Mrs. Roosevelt by C. Coco De Young • When Margo and her family are in danger of losing their house, Margo writes a letter to the first lady, Eleanor Roosevelt. Mrs. Roosevelt not only replies, but sends help in a surprising way.

Nothing to Fear by Jackie French Koller • Danny Garvey is a young Irish boy in the middle of the Great Depression. He shines shoes every day before school to help his mother with expenses. Will his family earn enough to keep their apartment, or will they end up homeless like so many others?

Red Scarf Girl by Ji-li Jiang • Ji-li Jiang is smart, young, and caught in the middle of China's Cultural Revolution. Will she testify against her father to remain in good standing with the government, or refuse to testify and give up everything she has ever dreamed of? Find out in this book for advanced readers!

Snow Treasure by Marie McSwigan • It's up to Peter and his friends to save Norway's gold from the Nazis. But first they have to find the secret cave, get past the Nazi troops, and devise a plan to get the gold to safety.

SOS Titanic by Eve Bunting • Barry, a young Irish boy, is on the ill-fated *Titanic* on his way to America to meet parents he doesn't even remember. Will he survive the revenge of the Flynn brothers and the sinking of the *Titanic*? Find out when you step aboard for the voyage of a lifetime!

Trouble River by Betsy Byars • Dewey's raft is on its way down Trouble River. His grandma better hold on tight, because their life just may depend on how fast they can escape.

The Watsons Go to Birmingham—1963 by Christopher Paul Curtis • The Weird Watsons, as Kenny refers to his family, are taking a trip to Birmingham, Alabama. Momma has the trip all planned out, but even she can't predict the events that will take place before this adventure ends.

Answer Keys

Page 14

1. 18 DKr
2. 480 DKr
3. 24 DKr
4. 10 DKr
5. 8 DKr
6. 20 DKr
7. 34 DKr
8. 120 DKr
9. 96 DKr
10. 40 DKr
11. 56 DKr
12. 28 DKr

Page 20

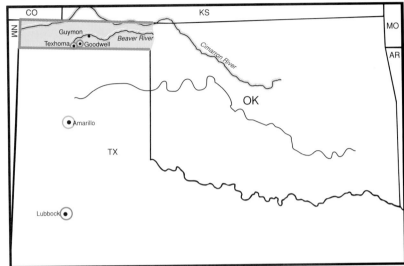

2. Student responses will vary. Accept all reasonable responses.
8. Student responses will vary. Accept all reasonable responses.

Page 15

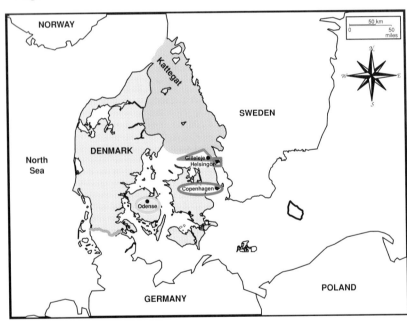

1. northeast
2. Denmark
3. Student responses may vary. Possible answers: plane, boat, catamaran, surfboard, jetski
4. Student responses will vary. Accept all reasonable responses.

Page 19

1. d
2. b
3. a
4. e
5. c

Page 25

1. $200.00
2. $20.00
3. $200.00
4. $40.00
5. $460.00
6. No, he still owes $60.00.
7. Answers will vary. Possible answers include that Mr. Turner could join with the Logans and shop where the prices are fair, or he could borrow more money from Mr. Montier to make it through the next year.

Page 26

I.

1. body
2. peanut butter
3. classroom
4. Logans
5. goose
6. Cassie
7. waddle
8. Little Man
9. watermelon
10. sharecropper

II.

The Sir Isaac "Fig" Newton!

Page 31

Answers may vary. Accept reasonable responses.
1. Use your time wisely. Do not waste time.
2. It is healthy to go to bed early and wake up early; you will feel better and you will do better.
3. Don't waste today wishing for tomorrow.
4. Do not spend too much time talking about doing something; do it.
5. It is better to be good at doing things than it is to be good at talking about them.

Page 32

1. 6:37 A.M.
2. 12:11 P.M.
3. 5½ hours
4. 2:14 P.M.
5. 8:11 P.M.
6. 15½ hours
7. 3:21 A.M.
8. 9:21 A.M.
9. 15½ hours
10. 3, 4, 18
11. 1, 15, 16
12. 2, 15

Page 36

1. about 2,333 fathoms
2. 1,200 feet
3. 2,133 fathoms
4. 4,729 fathoms
5. about 3,699 fathoms
6. about 2,166 fathoms
7. 505 fathoms
8. 1,606 fathoms
9. 2,980 fathoms
10.

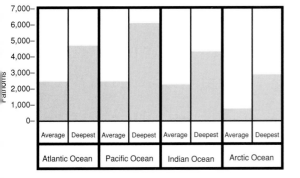

Page 37

1. $2.00; 14,000 maravedis
2. $4.00; 28,000 maravedis
3. $2.25; 15,750 maravedis
4. $9.00; 63,000 maravedis
5. $6.35; 44,450 maravedis
6. $21.45; 150,150 maravedis
7. 63,000 maravedis; $9.00
8. 56,000 maravedis; $8.00
9. 42,000 maravedis; $6.00
10. 56,000 maravedis; $8.00
11. 35,000 maravedis; $5.00
12. 28,000 maravedis; $4.00

Page 38

1.

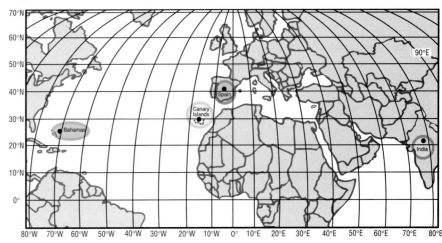

2. Canary Islands: 30°N and 20°N
   Bahamas: 30°N and 20°N
   India: 40°N and 0°
3. Yes
4. Canary Islands: 20°W and 10°W
   Bahamas: 80°W and 70°W
   India: 60°E and 90°E
5. No
6. No; Student responses will vary.

Page 42

1. c
2. k
3. e
4. f
5. d
6. a
7. i
8. l
9. g
10. j
11. b
12. h

Page 43

@ = n	8 = s
% = f	2 = d
& = o	4 = t
# = e	5 = a
* = b	

Students' responses to the meanings of the quotes may vary. Possible answers are listed.
1. "One always needs a final friend." When a sailor dies, he needs a friend to sew him into his hammock and throw his body overboard.
2. "I shall break them to my will." I will treat the crew harshly until they do what I say.
3. "Beware your friend, Miss Doyle, beware him." Be careful of Captain Jaggery, who you think is your friend, because he is not truly a friend.
4. "As a man he claims our mercy." Because Mr. Cranick is a human being, he deserves to be taken care of.
5. "No one ranks for creative genius like a sailor shirking work." Sailors are geniuses when it comes to thinking of ways to avoid doing work.
6. "Keep your eyes steady on the ropes. Don't you look down. Or up." You must focus on the ropes you are climbing. Do not look up or down or you will fall.
7. "One shipmate helps another." I am willing to help you because you are one of the crew.
8. "Sweet are the uses of adversity." When things are not going well, I can take advantage of the situation by having the crew do extra work.

Page 44

1. 9:30 A.M.
2. 12:00 A.M.
3. 7:00 P.M.
4. 6:30 A.M.
5. 12:30 P.M.
6. 2:00 A.M.
7. 5 bells after afternoon watch
8. forenoon watch or 8 bells after morning watch
9. 2 bells after first dog watch
10. 6 bells after midwatch
11. 7 bells after night watch
12. 3 bells after morning watch

Page 48

August 19, 1858—E. Nesbit, the author of *The Phoenix and the Carpet,* was born.

August 1876—Alexander Graham Bell received the first one-way long distance telephone call.

1879—Thomas Alva Edison invented the incandescent lamp.

September 6, 1901—President William McKinley was shot by an assassin.

September 7, 1901—The Boxer Rebellion was settled, ending the yearlong fighting in China.

September 14, 1901—Theodore Roosevelt became the youngest president of the United States.

December 17, 1903—The Wright brothers made the world's first flight in an airplane they invented and built.

August 3, 1904—Captain Thomas Scott Baldwin flew the *California Arrow,* a motor-driven balloon.

April 18, 1906—San Francisco experienced one of the worst earthquakes in the history of the United States.

September 22, 1909—Fung Joe Guey, a young Chinese flier, built and flew his own flying machine.

Page 49

1. gingerbread men cookies
2. milk
3. turkey sandwiches
4. lemonade
5. grapes
6–10. Students' answers will vary. Accept all reasonable responses.

Page 50

1. 29$\frac{1}{2}$
2. 29, 30, or 31
3. 13
4. 12
5. 383
6. 365
7. 4,637 years old
8. 2,045 years old

Page 54
Part I.

1. Sunrise
2. Early morning
3. Late in the day
4. Around noon
5–8. Students' answers will vary. Accept all reasonable responses.

Page 55
Part I.

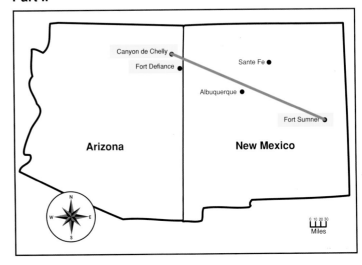

3. about 30 miles
4. about 270 miles
5. about 4 miles

Part II.

Students' answers may vary. Possible answers: Canyon de Chelly is where Bright Morning and her people lived before they were forced to move; Fort Defiance is where the soldiers who forced Bright Morning's people off their land were from; Fort Sumner is where the Navaho were taken and imprisoned for four years.

Page 59

1. Harrison Eddie Patrick
2. Doug Tennant
3. Chug Cross
4. Roy Breed
5. Bud Caldwell

Bud is named *Sleepy* by the bandmembers because he slept until 12:30 in the afternoon and *LaBone* because he is so slim.

Page 60

1. Kentland, Illinois, May 10, 1911
2. Loogootee, Indiana, May 16, 1911
3. Sturgis, Michigan, August 30, 1912
4. Gary, Indiana, June 13, 1912
5. Flint, Michigan, August 11, 1911
6. Idlewild, Michigan, May 2, 1936
7. Preston, Indiana, June 4, 1936
8. Chicago, Illinois, March 19, 1932